MEDITATION ON OM
AND
MANDUKYA UPANISHAD

D1673225

MEDITATION ON OM AND MANDUKYA UPANISHAD

Sri Swami Sivananda

Published by
THE DIVINE LIFE SOCIETY
P.O. SHIVANANDANAGAR—249 192
Distt. Tehri-Garhwal, Uttarakhand, Himalayas, India
www.sivanandaonline.org, www.dlshq.org

First Edition: 1941
Tenth Edition: 2018

[1000 Copies]

ISBN 81-7052-043-6
ES 103

PRICE: ₹ 60/-

Published by Swami Padmanabhananda for
The Divine Life Society, Shivanandanagar, and printed by
him at the Yoga-Vedanta Forest Academy Press,
P.O. Shivanandanagar, Distt. Tehri-Garhwal, Uttarakhand,
Himalayas, India
For online orders and Catalogue visit : dlsbooks.org

Om

Dedicated to

Ekakshara of the Gita

Pranava of the Vedas, Symbol of Brahman

Satnam Ek-Omkar of Guru Nanak

The Word of the Bible

The Mystic Word of Power

The Majestic Word

The Source, Support for Everything

Bestower of Immortality

Om

PRAYER TO OM

ओङ्कारं बिन्दुसंयुक्तं नित्यं ध्यायन्ति योगिनः ।
कामदं मोक्षदं चैव ओङ्करय नमो नमः ।।

Omkaram bindu samyuktam
        nityam dhyayanti yoginah,
Kamadam mokshadam chaiva
        omkaraya namo namah.

The yogins always meditate upon *Omkara* which has an *Anusvara* (denoted by a point) on it. This *Omkara* is the bestower of all desires and salvation. We bow down to the Supreme *Omkara*.

GURU VANDANA

Sri Vyasa Bhagavan Namostute,
Jaya Vishnu Avatara Namostute,
Sri Badarayana Namostute,
Jaya Krishna Dvaipayana Namostute.
Sri Sankaracharya Namostute,
Jaya Jagad Guru Namostute,
Advaitacharya Namostute,
Jaya Sankar Avatara Namostute.
Sri Dattatreya Namostute,
Jaya Sri Avadhuta Guru Namostute.
Sri Guru Deva Datta Namostute,
Jaya Trimurti Avatara Namostute.

GURU SMARANAM

Sri Natesa Saranam, Saranam Sri Venkatesa
Sri Sankaracharya Saranam,
Saranam Sri Vyasa Bhagavan,
Sri Dattatreya Saranam, Saranam Sri Radhe Krishna,
Sri Sita Rama Saranam, Saranam Sri Hanumantha.

GURU PRARTHANA

Sri Vyasabhagavan, Vyasabhagavan,
Vyasabhagavan Pahimam,
Sri Badarayana, Badarayana, Badarayana Rakshamam.
Sri Sankaracharya, Sankaracharya,
Sankaracharya Pahimam,

Sri Vedanta Guru, Vedanta Guru,
Vedanta Guru Rakṣhamam.
Sri Dattatreya, Dattatreya, Dattatreya Pahimam,
Sri Datta Guru, Datta Guru, Datta Guru Rakshamam.
Sri Sita Rama, Sita Rama, Sita Rama Pahimam,
Sri Hanumantha, Hanumantha,
Hanumantha Rakshamam.

OMKARA SMARANA STOTRA

ॐ स्मरणात् कीर्तनाद्वापि श्रवणाच्च जपादपि ।
ब्रह्म तत्प्राप्यते नित्यमोमित्येतत्परायणम् ।।१।।

1. That Supreme Brahman is attained by the devoted contemplation, hearing, Japa and Sankirtan of Om at all times.

ॐ इति स्मरणेनैव ब्रह्मज्ञानं परावरम् ।
तदेकमोक्षसिद्धिं च तदेवामृतमश्नुते ।।२।।

2. By the mere thought of Om one attains the highest Brahma Jnana, the state of final Liberation and Immortality.

तैलधारमिवाच्छिन्नं दीर्घघंटानिनादवत् ।
उपास्यं प्रणवस्याग्रं यस्तं वेद स वेदवित् ।।३।।

3. He who meditates on the Pranava in a continuous stream of thought like that of oil poured from one vessel to another or the continuous sound of a bell, such a man should be considered as the knower of Vedas.

बुद्धतत्त्वेन धीदोषशून्येनैकान्तवासिना ।
दीर्घं प्रणवमुच्चार्य मनोराज्यं विजीयते ।।४।।

4. By the long repetition of Om, the knower of the Supreme Reality whose refuge is solitude overcomes the wandering of the mind due to the taint in the intellect.

नासाग्रे बुद्धिमारोप्य हस्तपादौ च संयमेत् ।
मनः सर्वत्र संगृह्य ॐकारं तत्र चिन्तयेत् ॥५॥

5. Concentrating on the tip of the nose with hands and feet controlled, the mind withdrawn from all activities, one should meditate on *Omkara*, the *Pranava*.

ॐ इत्येकाक्षरध्यानात् विष्णुर्विष्णुत्वमासवान् ।
ब्रह्मा ब्रह्मत्वमापन्नः शिवतामभवत् शिवः ॥६॥

6. By the meditation on the monosyllable Om, Vishnu attains the status of Vishnu; Brahma attains Brahmahood and Siva becomes Siva.

QUINTESSENCE OF VEDANTA

(Attributes of Brahman)

अद्वैत अखण्ड अकर्ता अभोक्ता
असंग असक्त निर्गुण निर्लिप्त
चिदानन्दरूपः शिवोऽहं शिवोऽहम् ॥१॥

1. Advaita, Akhanda, Akarta, Abhokta,
   Asanga, Asakta, Nirguna, Nirlipta,
   Chidanandarupah Sivoham Sivoham.

अव्यक्तं अनन्त अमृत आनन्द
अचल अमर अक्षर अव्यय
चिदानन्दरूपः शिवोऽहं शिवोऽहम् ॥२॥

2. Avyakta, Ananta, Amrita, Ananda,
   Achala, Amara, Akshara, Avyaya,
   Chidanandarupah Sivoham Sivoham.

अशब्द अस्पर्श अरूप अगंध
अप्राण अमन अतीन्द्रिय अदृश्य
चिदानन्दरूपः शिवोऽहं शिवोऽहम् ॥३॥

3. Asabda, Asparsa, Arupa, Agandha,
   Aprana, Amana, Atindriya, Adrisya,
   Chidanandarupah Sivoham Sivoham.

सत्यं शिवं शुभं सुन्दरं कान्तं
सच्चिदानन्द सम्पूर्ण सुखशान्तं
चिदानन्दरूपः शिवोऽहं शिवोऽहम् ॥४॥

4. Satyam, Sivam, Subham, Sundaram, Kantam,
   Sat-chit-ananda, Sampurna, Sukha, Santam,
   Chidanandarupah Sivoham Sivoham.

चेतन चैतन्य चिद्घन चिन्मय
चिदाकाश चिन्मात्र सन्मात्र तन्मय
चिदानन्दरूपः शिवोऽहं शिवोऽहम् ॥५॥

5. Chetana, Chaitanya, Chidghana, Chinmaya,
   Chidakasa, Chinmatra, Sanmatra, Tanmaya,
   Chidanandarupah Sivoham Sivoham.

अमल विमल निर्मल अचल
अवाङ्मनोगोचर अक्षर निश्चल
चिदानन्दरूपः शिवोऽहं शिवोऽहम् ॥६॥

6. Amala, Vimala, Nirmala, Achala,
   Avangmanogochara, Akshara, Nischala,
   Chidananda-rupah Sivoham Sivoham.

नित्य निरुपाधिक निरतिशय आनन्द
निराकार ह्रींकार ॐकार कूटस्थ
चिदानन्दरूपः शिवोऽहं शिवोऽहम् ॥७॥

7. Nitya, Nirupadhika, Niratisaya Ananda,
   Nirakara, Hrimkara, Omkara, Kutastha,
   Chidanandarupah Sivoham Sivoham.

पूर्ण परब्रह्म प्रज्ञान आनन्द
साक्षी दृष्टा तुरीय विज्ञान आनन्द
चिदानन्दरूपः शिवोऽहं शिवोऽहम् ॥८॥

8. Purna Para-brahma, Prajnana Ananda,
   Sakshi, Drishta, Turiya, Vijnana Ananda,
   Chidanandarupah Sivoham Sivoham.

सत्यं ज्ञानमनन्तं आनन्दं

सच्चिदानन्द स्वयं ज्योतिप्रकाश

चिदानन्दरूपः शिवोऽहं शिवोऽहम् ॥९॥

9. Satyam, Jnanam, Anantam, Anandam,
   Sat-chit-ananda, Turiya, Vijnana Ananda,
   Chidanandarupah Sivoham Sivoham.

कैवल्य केवल कूटस्थ ब्रह्म

शुद्ध सिद्ध बुद्ध सच्चिदानन्द

चिदानन्दरूपः शिवोऽहं शिवोऽहम् ॥१०॥

10. Kaivalya, Kevala, Kutastha, Brahma,
    Suddha, Siddha, Buddha, Sat-chit-ananda,
    Chidanandarupah Sivoham Sivoham.

निर्दोष निर्मल विमल निरंजन

नित्य निराकार निर्गुण निर्विकल्प

चिदानन्दरूपः शिवोऽहं शिवोऽहम् ॥११॥

11. Nirdosha, Nirmala, Vimala, Niranjana,
    Nitya, Nirakara, Nirguna, Nirvikalpa,
    Chidanandarupah Sivoham Sivoham.

आत्मा ब्रह्मस्वरूप चैतन्य पुरुष

तेजोमय आनन्द तत्त्वमसिलक्ष्य

चिदानन्दरूपः शिवोऽहं शिवोऽहम् ॥१२॥

12. Atma Brahma Svarupa, Chaitanya Purusha
    Tejomaya Ananda 'Tat-tvam-asi' Lakshya,
    Chidanandarupah Sivoham Sivoham.

सोऽहं शिवोऽहं अहं ब्रह्मास्मि महावाक्य
शुद्धसच्चिदानन्द पूर्ण परब्रह्म
चिदानन्दरूपः शिवोऽहं शिवोऽहम् ॥१३॥

13. 'Soham' 'Sivoham' 'Aham Brahmasmi' Mahavakya,
    Suddha Satchidananda, Purna Para-brahma,
    Chidananda rupah Sivoham Sivoham.

NIRGUNA SONG

निर्गुणोऽहं निष्कलोऽहं निर्ममोऽहं निश्चलः ।
नित्यशुद्धो नित्यबुद्धो निर्विकारो निष्क्रियः ॥१॥

निर्मलोऽहं केवलोऽहं एकमेव अद्वितीयः ।
भासुरोऽहं भास्करोऽहं नित्यतृप्तो चिन्मयः ।

पूर्णकामो पूर्णरूपो पूर्णकालो पूर्णदिक् ।
आदिमध्य–अन्तहीनो जननमरण–वर्जितः ॥३॥

सर्वकर्ता सर्वभोक्ता सर्वसाक्षी स्वयमस्म्यहम् ।
सर्वव्यापी द्वयातीतो नास्ति किञ्चन काप्यहो ॥४॥

INTRODUCTION

The Infinite is Bliss. The Infinite only is Bliss. The Infinite is Brahman, the Atman, and the Supreme Self. The Infinite is the Absolute. The Infinite is *Bhuma*, the unconditioned, that is beyond time, space and causation. The Infinite is Immortality. Where one sees nothing else, hears nothing else, understands nothing else there is Infinity. The Infinite abides in Its own greatness. The Infinite is Supreme Peace. The Infinite is Fearlessness. The Infinite is Existence Absolute, Knowledge Absolute, Bliss Absolute. The Infinite is All-full and indivisible. The Infinite is Self-existent, self-contained and Self-luminous. The Infinite alone is real. The Infinite alone exists in the three periods of time. You must search, understand and realise the Infinite.

Brahman is infinite. Brahman is the only reality. Brahman is independent and self-existent. The finite cannot be self-consistent, real and self-dependent. The finite depends for its existence upon something else, namely Brahman, the Absolute. People generally raise the question why and how if the Brahman is the only Reality, the finite appears at all? You cannot understand how the appearances come out of Brahman and are absorbed into It. You can understand this only when you get Knowledge of the Self. This is a transcendental question, *Atiprasna*. The finite intellect that is conditioned in time, space and causation cannot find out a solution for a thing which is beyond time, space and causation. Do not rack your brain any more on this point.

Brahman or the Absolute is eternally perfect and good. The evil is due to illusion. It is illusion that makes you see evil. Get Knowledge of Brahman, the Self. The illusion and evil will vanish and you will behold the Self only everywhere.

There is no bliss in anything finite. Where one sees or hears or understands something else, that is finite. The finite is perishable. The finite is conditioned in time, space end causation. The finite is mortality. The finite is creation of *Maya*. The finite is unreal. The finite is mere appearance. The finite has no independent existence. The finite depends upon the Infinite for its own relative existence. The finite can never be apart from the Infinite.

Some ignorant people only say that Vedanta preaches immorality, hatred and pessimism. This is a very sad mistake. Vedanta does not preach either immorality or even indifference to morality. The realisation of Brahman is not possible for the immoral. An aspirant who has ethical perfection and who is endowed with the four means, can become a student of Vedanta. How can you expect an aspirant who possesses discrimination, dispassion, serenity, self-restraint, forbearance, endurance, faith, one-pointed mind and a burning desire for liberation to lead an immoral life? It is quite absurd. Vedanta wants you to destroy selfish love and passion for the body and to develop pure, disinterested, cosmic love, the magnanimous divine *Prem*. It never preaches pessimism but it preaches the pinnacle of optimism. It preaches "give up this little illusory pleasure, and you will get eternal and infinite bliss. Kill this little 'I', and you will become one with the Infinite, you will become Immortal. Give up this illusory world and you will get the vast domain of Supreme peace, the Kingdom of God." Is this pessimism? Certainly not. It is wonderful optimism.

Vedanta wants you to give up *Moha* for body, wife, children and property. Vedanta wants you to abandon all worldly desires, cravings and longings for worldly objects. Vedanta wants you to eradicate the desire for power, name and fame. Vedanta wants you to break all ties and connections with the world. Vedanta wants you to cut off ruthlessly all worldly attachments by the sword of discrimination.

Rise above desires. Abandon your beggarly attitude of mind. Feel the majesty of your Self. There is neither desire nor *vasanas* in the Self. It is ever pure. It is all-full and self-contained. Identify yourself with the glorious Self. Then all desires will die. Then all desires will be fulfilled. This is the secret of the fulfilment of desires. Then Nature will obey you. You can command the elements. All the eight *Siddhis* and the nine *Riddhis* will roll under your feet. They will stand with folded hands to carry out your behests. This is the sublime teaching of Vedanta.

Lord Jesus commanded the waves to subside. They obeyed immediately. Shams Tabriez commanded the sun to come down a bit. The sun obeyed. Nimbarka commanded the sun not to move beyond the line of the *Neem* tree that was in front of his house. The sun carried out his behest immediately. Jnana Dev commanded the wall and the Masjid to move. They obeyed at once. Visvamitra said: "Let there be a third world for Trisanku." Then and there a world was created. Akalkot Swamiji commanded: "Let this dead man come back to life." At once the dead man rose up from the ground with new life. These sages were absolutely free from selfish desires. They simply willed at times to do good to the humanity. Everything came to pass instantaneously.

Vedanta, the Knowledge of the Self, is not the sole property of Sannyasins or recluses who live in forests or caves of the Himalayas. Study the Upanishads and you will find that many *Kshatriya* kings, who were very busy in their daily affairs of life, were in possession of *Brahma-Jnana*. They gave instructions to Brahmin priests even. Pravahana Jaivali the king of Panchala taught the *Panchagni-vidya*, the knowledge of five fires to Gautama and his son, Svetaketu. Sukadev had to go to king Janaka to have confirmation of his Knowledge and Realisation. He was tested by Janaka in his Durbar.

You must be practical Vedantin. Mere theorising and lecturing is only intellectual gymnastics and lingual warfare.

This will not suffice. If Vedanta is not practicable, no theory is of any value. You must put Vedanta in daily practice in every action. Vedanta teaches oneness or unity of Self. You must radiate love to one and all. The spirit of Vedanta must be ingrained in your cells and tissues, nerves and bones. It must become part and parcel of your nature. You must think of unity, speak of unity and act in unity. If you deliver a thrilling lecture on the platform on Vedanta and say, "I am the all, I am the one Self in all, there is nothing but myself," and show in action the next moment a different attitude of selfishness and separateness, you will not produce any impression on the public. You will be called a dry Vedantin only. Nobody will care for you.

See how king Janaka lived. He lived the life of a practical Vedantin while ruling his kingdom. You cannot conceive any man busier than King Janaka. He was ruling over millions of people and yet he was a sage, deep thinker, profound philosopher and a practical Vedantin. He had no attachment to his property or body or his family people. He shared what he had with others. He moved with all. He had equal vision and a balanced mind. He led a very busy life amidst luxuries. He was not a bit affected by external influences. He always kept up a serene mind. He held discussions with various sages, on transcendental matters. That is the reason why he still lives in our hearts.

If a Yogi or a Sannyasin, who is able to keep up serenity of mind while living in a cave in the forest, complains of disturbance of mind when he lives in the bustle of a city, he has no control of mind. He has no inner spiritual strength. He is not a practical Vedantin. He has no Self-realisation. He has not attained the goal of life. He is still within the domain of *Maya*. A real Yogi or a practical Vedantin is one who can keep perfect calmness of mind while performing intense activity amidst the bustle of a city. This is the central teaching of the Gita. Lord Krishna says, 'Remember me at all time and fight.' Lord Krishna imparted this instruction to Arjuna in the battlefield.

Though Arjuna was despondent in the beginning, he gained spiritual strength and fought in the battlefield with perfect tranquillity of mind. He became a practical Vedantin eventually.

If you can maintain, when you are performing intense activity, serenity of mind which cannot be ruffled, balance of mind which can never be disturbed, whatever happens, you have made considerable progress in the spiritual path. This indicates that you possess immense inner spiritual strength.

A Collector of a district saw a sick patient on the roadside in a dying condition. He was a very sympathetic man. He carried the patient to the neighbouring hospital on his own shoulders. Look at his feeling of oneness. He is a practical Vedantin whether he knows Upanishad or not. Many people and even many Sannyasins say, "Mahatma Gandhiji is a simple Karma Yogi only. He is not a Vedantin." There is no practical Vedantin greater than Gandhiji. He lived in every moment of his life, the life of a practical Vedantin. He lives for the well-being of the world only. He is the nerve-centre for this world. He is one with all. He embraces all with pure love. Self-sacrifice, service, non-violence, truthfulness, purity, unity are his creed. But he never puts on a label of a Vedantin. He never advertises, "I am Brahman—*Aham Brahmasmi.*"

The sun, the flowers, the Ganga, the sandal tree, the fruit-bearing trees, the cows—all teach practical Vedanta to the world. They live for serving the humanity in a disinterested spirit. The sun radiates its light alike over a cottage of a peasant and a palace of a king. The flowers waft their fragrance to all without expecting anything. The cool, refreshing waters of the Ganga are drunk by all. The sandal tree wafts its aroma even to the man who cuts it with an axe. The fruit-bearing trees behave in the same manner. They please the gardener who nourished them as well as the man who cuts them. The cows live to nourish babies, the children, the invalids and the convalescents. Imagine for a moment that the world is devoid of cows for six months or the race of cows has become

21

extinct. How miserable and weak you will become! The rate of mortality will increase considerably. The world will abound with anaemic patients. O selfish ignorant man, learn lessons from these practical Vedantins and become wise.

Vedanta is very practical. It does not preach an impossible ideal. Vamadev, Jadabharata, Sankara and many others have realised the truth of Vedanta. You can also realise it if you will. What is wanted is regular and constant practice. You must have perfect faith in the utterances of the Srutis and in the words of your Guru. You must have perfect faith in yourself first.

There is neither birth nor death for you. Thou art the immortal undecaying Self. *Maya* deludes you and you identify yourself with the perishable body. You foolishly imagine that you are subject to birth and death. Free yourself from the clutches of Maya. Soar high in the realms of Supreme Peace and reach the abode of Immortality through purification and meditation.

Sri Sankara, the great propounder of Advaita philosophy has said that the world is an illusion and the goal of man is to find the Reality behind the phenomenon. Plato also denied that the world was a reality. Even in the West, many philosophers have said that the world is mere an appearance and the noumenon only is the solid Reality.

The 'Over soul' of the Western philosophers is the Brahman of the Upanishads the Atman of the Vedantins. The Supreme Soul, the *Paramatman* which is the support for the individual soul is the 'Over soul.' The 'Over soul' is the 'substance' of Spinoza or the 'Thing in itself' of Kant. The essence of Vedanta has slowly been infiltrated into the minds of Western philosophers and they have accepted now the existence of one eternal principle or Self which is distinct from body and mind.

To look for the God without, abandoning the God within, is like going in quest of conch-shells after giving up the precious diamond on the hand. If you cannot find Him in your heart you will not find Him anywhere else. Search Him within in the innermost recesses of the heart. He is subtler than the subtlest. Make the lotus of your heart as pure as possible. Withdraw the fuel of desires and extinguish the fire of *Sankalpas*. Realise the Truth now through your higher mind. Enjoy the perennial joy of Divine Bliss.

A rich man keeps his valuable jewels in an iron safe that is kept in the innermost chamber of his bungalow. One has to pass through five compartments before he reaches the compartment in which the iron safe is placed. Five walls screen the iron safe. Even so this most valuable jewel of the Atman is placed in the innermost recesses of your heart. Five veils cover this Atman. The five veils are the *Annamaya*, *Pranamaya, Manomaya, Vijnanamaya* and *Anandamaya Kosas*. You must tear these five veils if you want to approach the Atman. In other words, you will have to pass through the five compartments formed by the five *Kosas* if you want to get at the jewel of the Atman.

You cannot separate the particles of sugar that are mixed with sand or dust; but an ant can separate them very easily. So also if you want to taste the nectar of Immortality or enjoy the Atmic Bliss, if you want to separate the Atman from the five sheaths, you must become an ant, i.e., you must kill your egoism, pride and vanity and develop humility.

Mind, body, *Prana* and the senses are parts of the phenomenal world. There are two aspects of the Truth, viz., static and dynamic. The static aspect is the *Trigunatita Ananta Brahman*, the impersonal God. The dynamic aspect is the personal God, *Isvara*. World is God in motion. It is the dynamic aspect. Power and spirit are one. Existence is unmanifested Brahman. Expression or motion or manifestation is Saguna Brahman. Brahman seen through the veil of *Maya* is *Isvara*, personal God. This phenomenal appearance is an illusion. You cannot dismiss the phenomenal world as merely imaginary and yet cannot treat it as real. *Maya* is neither *Sat* (real) nor *Asat* (unreal) nor *Sat-asat*. It is an indescribable illusory power of God.

Believe in the glory of your own Self. "Thou Art That." Search, hear and understand. Reflect, meditate and realise this Immortal Atman. This Atman was never born and will never die. Abandon all superstitions and doubts. Scorch out all wrong *Samskaras* and wrong suggestions. Man or woman can realise the goal of Vedanta. Burn all false differences. There is no low, no high, no great, no small, no superior, no inferior, no animate, no inanimate. Behold your own Self everywhere. There is nothing but the Self.

Your individual will will become one with the cosmic will. You will have experience of cosmic consciousness. You will feel that all ears are your ears, all eyes your eyes, all mouths your mouths, all tongues your tongues, all hands your hands, all legs your legs and all minds your minds. This will be a magnanimous experience indeed. Words will fail to describe adequately the grandeur of this experience.

You cannot die, because you were never born. You are the immortal Atman. Birth and death are two false scenes in the unreal drama of *Maya*. They concern the physical sheath only, a false product formed by the combination of five elements. The ideas of birth and death are a mere superstition.

O Ye of little faith, wake up from your long sleep of ignorance. Get the knowledge of the Self. O wanderer in this quagmire of *Samsara*, go back to your original abode of eternal peace, the fountain of infinite joy and power, the spring of boundless ecstasy, the source of life, the origin of light and love, the immortal blissful Brahmic seat of illimitable splendour and pristine glory. Fill the mind with thoughts of the Self. Saturate your feelings with purity and divinity. Let the Light of lights shine in every hair on your body. Let the Infinite Godhead vibrate in every cell of your body. Let every breath sing the song of Infinity and eternity with *Soham*.

Vedanta is that sublime philosophy which teaches that the individual soul is identical with the Supreme Soul and removes the illusion of the *jiva*. Vedanta is the science of the Atman that helps the aspirants to eradicate fear, sorrow, grief, delusion and to realise the Self. Vedanta is that magnanimous philosophy which raises the ignorant *Jiva* to the sublime heights of Brahmanhood. Vedanta is the panacea for all human ailments. Vedanta is the sovereign specific for the disease of birth and death. Mere theorising of Vedantic principles will not do. You should become a practical Vedantin. You should do *Sadhana* in the prescribed lines. The *japa*, chanting and meditation on Om are the most important portions of the Vedantic Sadhana.

The state of *Turiya, Brahman*, the Atman and Om are one. Om is an embodiment of the essence of the whole of the Vedas. The Brahmins used the sacred monosyllable as the first and the last word of every religious ceremony. The whole essence of the Vedas is compressed in the symbol of Om. This symbol is endowed with occult powers of the highest character. Aspirants who tread the path of Vedanta repeat always mentally Om with *Bhava* and feeling and enjoy supreme Bliss from this mystic practice.

Again and again, sing the glory of Om. Apply your heart, mind and soul to the music of Om. Perform all actions as an adoration of the sacred *Pranava*. Live and move in Om. Make Om the centre of your dwelling place. Utter Om in each and every breath of the nose. Be ever wakeful in the bliss of Om. Melt the dream of this illusive world in the wakefulness of Om. Sink the pains and miseries of *Samsara* in the bliss of Om, the bliss of the Eternal, the Abode of Peace, Bliss and Joy.

Be a spiritual hero in the *Adhyatmic* battlefield. Become a brave, undaunting, spiritual soldier. The inner war with the mind, the senses, *Vasanas* and *Samskaras* is more terrible than the external war. Fight against the mind, the senses, the evil *Vasanas*, *Trishnas*, *Vrittis* and *Samskaras* boldly. Use the machine-gun of *Brahma-vichara* to explode the mind efficiently. Dive deep and destroy the under-currents of passion, greed, hatred, pride and jealousy through the submarine or torpedo of the *Japa* of Om. Soar high in the higher regions of bliss of the Self with the help of aeroplane of *Brahmakara-vritti*. Use the 'mines' of chanting of Om to explode the *Vasanas* that are hidden in the sea of the subconscious mind. Sometimes move the 'tanks' of discrimination to crush your ten enemies, the ten turbulent senses. Start the 'Divine League' and make friendship with your powerful allies, viz., dispassion, fortitude, endurance, serenity, self-restraint, to attack your enemy—mind. Throw the bomb of *Sivoham Bhavana* to destroy the big mansion of body and the ideas 'I am the body', 'I am the doer', 'I am the enjoyer'. Spread profusely the gas of *Sattva* to destroy your internal enemies, viz., *Rajas* and *Tamas* quickly. 'Black out' the mind by destroying the *Vrittis* or *Sankalpas* by putting out all the lights or bulbs of sensual objects so that the enemy-mind may not attack you. Fight closely against your enemy-mind with the bayonet of one-pointedness (*Samadhana*) to get hold of the priceless treasure of the Atmic Pearl. The joy of *Samadhi*, the Bliss of *Moksha*, the Peace of *Nirvana* are now yours, whoever you may be, in whatever clime you are born. Whatever might he your past life and history, work out your salvation. O Beloved Ram, with the help of the above means (*Sadhana*) come out victorious right now in this very second. Meditation on Om with *Bhava* and meaning leads to realisation of *Brahma-jnana*. This is the Vedantic *Sadhana*.

Think of nothing other than Om. Dedicate all your actions and movements for the sake of the Eternal. May Om be the solace of your life. May Om be the solace of your past, present and future. May you ever live drowned in the ecstasy of *Pranava*.

Sri Appayya Dikshit-Acharya has expounded the oldest Vedanta on modern lines. It is called *Sankhya Yoga* or *Anubhavadvaita* or Experiential Monism. He has written a number of works, but his *Pranava Rahasya* is important from this view point. It is in manuscript form. Much information on this mystic *Pranava* can be gathered from Sri Rama Gita (which forms a part of *Tattvasarayana* translated into English by Pundit G. Krishna Sastri and on which there is a Tamil commentary by Appayya Dikshit), *Anubhuti Mimamsa Bhashya Muktiratna* and *Jivachintamani*.

In this book, I have given all important items that are useful for all *Sadhakas*. The book is divided into 7 Chapters dealing with Philosophy of Om, Meditation on Om, Prayers, Songs and Kirtan on Om. Detailed lessons given in this book on Japa, meditation of Om will be of great help to all aspirants in their daily *Sadhana*. At the end I have added the exhaustive notes and commentary on Mandukya Upanishad, the most important of all the major or classical Upanishads.

Mandukya Upanishad is an Upanishad of the Atharva Veda. It is one of the classical Upanishads. There are 12 *Mantras* in the Upanishad. Sri Gaudapadacharya, the *Parama Guru* the grand-preceptor of Sri Sankara has written a *Karika* on the Upanishad which is very illuminating and sublime.

The Upanishad takes its name after the seer of the Upanishad, Manduka. It is the shortest of the ten classical Upanishads. Among the Upanishads it is the most difficult. Sri Gaudapada has written 251 verses as the *Karika* to explain this most important Upanishad. Sri Sankara has written a commentary on both the Upanishad and *Karika*. Ananda Giri has written a *Tika* on the Upanishad, which gives a very good explanation of Sri Sankara's commentary.

The Upanishad is very terse. Without the help of this *Karika* you cannot have a comprehensive understanding of the *mantras*; you cannot get a clear insight into the system of thought or philosophy that is propounded in this unique Upanishad.

The Upanishad does not deal with rituals and *Upasana*. It does not contain any story or parable or dialogue. It deals with pure philosophy alone, with the metaphysical discussion of the Ultimate Reality, Brahman and the method of approach to the Truth. It is said in the Muktikopanishad: "The only means by which the final emancipation is attained is through Mandukya Upanishad alone which is enough for the salvation of all aspirants."

This short Upanishad gives the secret meaning of Om which is the name of Brahman. It gives an analysis of the three states of waking, dream and deep sleep. Through a study and clear grasp of these states, through proper understanding of Om and its right significance, you can find out the way to approach and realise Brahman.

Study Mandukya Upanishad. You will know all about Om and the four states, viz., waking state, dream state, deep sleep state and *Turiya* (the fourth)), Brahman.

May you all rest in the non-dual Brahman and taste the nectar of Immortality! May you all reach the fourth state of Bliss, *Turiya* by analysing the experiences of the waking, dream and deep sleep states! May you all have a comprehensive understanding of *Omkara* or *Pranava*, and the *Amatra*. May you all enter the soundless Om by transcending the sounds, "A", "U" and "M". May you all meditate on Om and attain the goal of life, the Ultimate Reality, *Sat-chit-ananda Para Brahman*. May the Om guide you. May this Om be your centre, ideal and goal. May the secrets and truths of this Mandukya Upanishad be revealed unto you. May the blessings of Sri Gaudapada, Sri Sankara and the seer of this Upanishad be upon you all!

Om! Om!! Om!!!

Swami Sivananda

26th February, 1940

CONTENTS

Chapter I: PHILOSOPHY OF OM

Chapter II: MEDITATION ON OM

Chapter III

Chapter IV

Chapter V: SONGS AND KIRTANS ON OM

Chapter VI: GARLAND OF OM

Chapter VII

MEDITATION ON OM
AND
MANDUKYA UPANISHAD

PHILOSOPHY OF OM

SYMBOL OF BRAHMAN

Para-brahman, that Eternal Highest Being, the abiding place of all that lives and moves, is beyond name and class. The Vedas have ventured to give a name to Him, in order that man may recognise and call Him. A newborn child has no name, but on receiving one he will answer to it. Men who are troubled by the afflictions of this world run to the Deity for refuge, and call Him by the name. When Brahman is invoked through the name, that which is hidden is revealed to the aspirant.

Brahman is the highest of all. Om is His name. So Om is to be adored. Om is everything. Om is the name or symbol of God, Isvara, Brahman. Om is your real name. Om covers all the threefold experience of man. Om stands for all phenomenal words. From Om this sense-universe has been projected. The world exists in Om and dissolves in Om. Om is formed by adding the letters A, U, M. 'A' represents the physical plane, 'U' represents the mental and the astral planes, the world of spirits, all heavens and 'M' represents all the deep sleep state and all that is unknown and beyond the reach of the intellect even in your waking. Om therefore represents all. Om is the basis of your life, thought and intelligence. All words that denote objects are centred in Om. Hence the whole world has come from Om, rests in Om and dissolves in Om. As soon as you sit for meditation, chant Om loudly 3 or 6 or 12 times. This will drive away all worldly thoughts from the mind and remove *Vikshepa* (tossing of the mind). Then take to mental repetition of Om.

The life of all words is vowels. A vowel is that which shines by itself. It can be pronounced by itself. A consonant is that which cannot be pronounced without the help of a vowel placed either before or after it. A consonant can be sounded with the aid of a vowel. Just as thy body depends for its very existence on the soul or the Atman, so also the consonants depend for their very pronunciation on the vowels. 'A' and 'U' are the parents of all other vowels in Sanskrit. Sanskrit possesses a large number of vowels than any other language in the world. All the letters of the alphabets of all languages are contained in this mysterious, sacred monosyllable—Om (AUM). Therefore, it is quite proper to regard Om as the symbol or name of Brahman.

Watch the breath. When you inhale, the sound 'so' is produced; when you exhale the sound 'ham' is produced. You are naturally uttering 'Soham,' 'I am He' or 'He am I,' along with every breath. The breath reminds you that you are in essence identical with the Supreme Self. In 'Soham,' 's' and 'h' are consonants. If you delete the consonants 's' and 'h' you get 'oam' or Om. Consonants have no independence of their own. They depend on vowels for their existence. 's' and 'h' represent the names and forms, or this universe which has only a phenomenal or relative or empirical or dependent existence. Om is the only solid reality. Om is the soul of your breath.

There is what is called *Pancha-santi*, five kinds of incantations, each ending with the word Santi, 'Peace.' Before each Santi there is the word Om. As such Om gives peace, calmness, tranquillity and serenity. This symbol brings the entire universe and all it contains in its span. It means something more, 'a' is the first letter of the alphabets and 'm' is the last syllable in Sanskrit. Thus 'a' and 'm' mean everything from A to Z. It is the alpha and omega of everything. It represents everything from beginning to end and since there is the other part 'u,' Om includes everything we can imagine and something more too. As such it is a fit symbol to be meditated upon. No other symbol can span so much in its embrace.

The sound produced in the flowing Ganga, the sound that is heard at a distance and that which proceeds from the bustle of a market, the sound that is produced when the fly wheel of an engine is set in motion, the sound that is caused when it rains, the sound that is produced when there is a conflagration of fire, when there is thunder, it is all Om only. You split any word, you find Om is there. Om is all-pervading like *Akasa*, like Brahman.

Om is the symbol of Brahman. It is the word of power. It is the sacred monosyllable. It is the essence of all the Vedas. It is the boat to take you to the other shore of fearlessness and immortality. Meditate on Om with *bhava* and meaning. When you think or meditate on Om, you will have to think of Brahman, the thing signified by the symbol.

The word 'Om' is the most appropriate name of Brahman, the (Supreme Spirit). By its application, by its chanting, He becomes propitiated, as men by the use of their favourite names. It is emblematic of Brahman, as images are of material objects. When you hear the sound 'tree,' you at once understand that it has a root, stem, branches, leaves, flowers, fruits, etc. Similarly when you hear the sound 'Om' it denotes Sat-chit-ananda Brahman—Existence Absolute, Knowledge Absolute, Bliss Absolute. *Sabda* and *Artha* are inseparable. All collection of speech or words terminate in one sound Om. All the objects are denoted by sound and all sounds merge in Omkara. The whole universe comes out of Om and is absorbed in Om. Hence Om is very important. It should be worshipped. It should be chanted loudly. It should be repeated mentally with meaning and feeling. It should be meditated upon.

Why is Om taken as the symbol of Brahman? Can we not have any other word besides Om to represent Brahman, the solid Reality, the living Truth? Om is a mysterious and sacred syllable. Chant Om for one hour. Chant any other word

also for one hour. You will yourself feel the difference. There
is a real connection between Om, the symbol and Brahman,
the thing signified by the symbol Om. Thought and word are
inseparable. Om and Brahman are inseparable. When you
think of the name of your son Govind, the name will bring to
your memory the picture or image of your son. When you
think of the image of Om, the image will bring to your memory
Brahman the thing signified. There is intimate relationship
between the symbol Om and Brahman the thing signified.

Om is the common symbol. It will represent all the symbols of God, all symbols of religions, all cults and schools.
Just as a large-hearted spiritual man who is of catholic, liberal
nature without prejudice of any sort, represents all and becomes the supreme head of conference of world religions, so
also the common symbol Om, the basis of all sounds and all
languages, represents all names and becomes the head of
all names of God.

Prana vibrates. Air moves. Heat is generated. The
heated air strikes against the vocal cords in the larynx or the
sound box. Sound is produced. Sound is modified by its pas-
sage through palate, nose, tongue, teeth, lips, etc., and various kinds of sounds are produced. We have therefore
gutturals, labials, dentals, nasals, etc., etc. The larynx or wind
box, the trachea or the wind-pipe, palate, mouth, nose, teeth,
lips constitute the sound producing apparatus in this body.
Sound 'A' is guttural. This is the root sound. This is the key.
When this is pronounced, any part of the tongue or palate is
not touched. Sound 'U' rolls from the root to the very extremity
of the sounding board of the mouth. Sound 'M' is labial and
nasal. It comes from the end or extremity of the sounding
board of the mouth. It is produced by the closed lips. 'A' represents the beginning of the range of sound, 'U' represents the
middle, 'M' represents the end. Thus Om covers the whole
field of sounds and words. Om represents the entire range of
sounds and words. All words, all sounds are created in Om.
Om is a magical, mysterious, divine, gramophonic record of

all sounds and words. All words, all sounds, all languages proceed from Om. Therefore, Om is the right representative or natural symbol or womb of all sounds and words. Om is also the natural symbol of Brahman, the source of everything, the source for sounds, words, languages and all objects. Therefore worship Om. Live in Om. Meditate on Om. Merge in Om. Rejoice in Om.

IMPORTANCE OF OM

The vibration produced by chanting OM in the physical universe corresponds to the original vibration that first arose from the mouth of Hiranyagarbha the Karya-brahman. Hence Om is very important.

You will find in the Bible "in the beginning was the word, and the word was with God and the word was God." This is Om or the word of power. Even Adisesha or Sarasvati will not be able to exhaust the subject on this sacred' Mantra Om even if they have the water of the oceans as ink and all the trees of the world as pens. Volumes have been written in the Sanskrit language on the significance of Om, the sacred and the mysterious monosyllable. All Mantras begin with Om. The *Panchakshara* and *Ashtakshara Mantras* are contained in Om. All Vedas, all Vedanta, all the sacred scriptures of the Hindus are contained in Om. Om is the womb for everything. This world has come out of Om, exists in Om and dissolves in Om during the cosmic *Pralaya*. The creation itself is set in motion by the vibration of Om.

'Amen' is used by Christians at the end of their prayers. 'Amen' is used very frequently in the sacred Bible. Muslims use the word 'Ahmeen' during prayer. 'Amen' and 'Ahmeen' are all modifications of Om only. Om is the matrix of all sounds. When you experience acute agony or pain, you utter the long sound of 'hun' or 'hum' again and again and get some relief. 'Hun' or 'hum' is a modification of Om only. 'Hum' is partial utterance of Om which breaks on account of pain. When you suffer from pain you implore the mercy of the Lord by calling Him by His name. Laughter is nothing but a sound of many 'hums' repeatedly made.

When the child cries or weeps, it utters 'un' or 'aung.' 'Un' or 'aung' is a modification of Om only. As the child's organ of speech is not well-developed it utters Om unintelligibly. Even when the child weeps it repeats God's name. When the washerman washes his clothes he utters repeatedly 'hung' 'hung.' This gives him relief. He does not feel exhaustion or fatigue. He unconsciously repeats God's name and derives power, joy, peace and strength from within. The gurgling sounds produced in the bowels on account of flatulence, the whistling sound of the railway engine, the murmur of the running brooks, the sound of thunder, the howling of jackals, the roaring of lion, the sound of the mills and the factories are Om only. The sound of landslides, heavy rush of wind, the bustle of the city and that of the rainfall are Om only. You will clearly understand now that man utters Om, the name of the Lord or Brahman fully or partially, consciously or unconsciously at all times. If he utters with *bhava* and feeling he will realise quickly his own essential divine nature.

All colours are centred in the eye; all tastes are centred in the tongue; all touches are centred in the skin; all sounds are centred in the ear; all scents are centred in the nose; all senses are centred in the mind; all minds are centred in Om or Brahman, the Supreme Self, the Support for everything.

The humming of bees, the sweet melody of the nightingale, the seven tunes in music (Sa, Re, Ga, Ma, Pa, Dha, Ni and Sa), the sound of the *Mridanga* and kettle-drum, the lute and the flute, the roaring of the lion, the singing of the lover, the neighing of horses, the hissing of the cobra, the clapping of the audience when an orator delivers his peroration—all are emanations from Omkara only. Om is the embodiment of the Vedas.

All languages and sounds come out of Om. The essence of the four Vedas is Om only. A, U, M cover the whole range of sound vibrations. 'A' starts from the root of the tongue. 'U' proceeds from the middle. And 'M' comes from the end by closing the lips. He who chants or repeats Om really repeats the sacred books of the whole world. Om is the source or the womb for all religions and scriptures of different parts of the world. Om, Amen and Ahmeen are all one. They represent the Truth, Brahman, the one Existence. There is no worship without Om. Om is both *saguna* and *nirguna*, *sakara* and *nirakara*.

Pranava or Om is the greatest of all Mantras. It bestows directly liberation. All Mantras begin with Om. Every Upanishad begins with Om. Gayatri begins with Om. The oblations that are offered to the various Gods are preceded by the chanting of Om. The Archanas, viz., *Ashtottari* (108), *Trisati* (300) and *Sahasra* (1000) are also preceded by the *Pranava*. The greatness of the *Omkara* cannot be described by anybody. Even Parvati, Adisesha and great sages failed to describe the greatness of *Pranava*. There is Om in every sound.

Om is an auspicious trade mark of Sannyasins and Vedantins who deal with the trade of dissemination of spiritual knowledge to the world at large. It is written on the front wall of every *Ashram* of a Sannyasin. Om is used in the form of invocating or addressing in prayer or supplication. Om is the formula of imperative prayer which transmits a' certain grace or virtue to the person over whom it is pronounced. Votaries of Om write Om first before they try to start a letter.

BENEFITS OF OM

Rishis and sages of yore who have attained Self-realisation have experienced the mysterious effects of repetition or chanting of Om. They having made long researches and experiments on Om and its vibrations, meditated on OM for a considerable period and have then given to the world Om as the right symbol of Brahman. This is not a hocus-pocus work or a juggler's trick. This is authoritative assertion of the seers (Apta Vakyam). Om served as a beaconlight or light-house or a safe boat for them when they sailed in the turbulent and deep unnavigable waters of this ocean of *Samsara*. Through Om they ascended safely to the summit of the hill of *Nirvikalpa Samadhi,* the knowledge of the Self, Brahma Jnana. You can safely rely on their teachings.

There is a mysterious inscrutable force (Achintyasakti) in Om. This force tears the veils, destroys desires, cravings and egoism and takes the aspirant to Brahman. It raises the *Brahmakara Vritti* from the *sattvic* mind, annihilates the *Mula-ajnana* and helps the meditator to rest in his own *Sat-chit-ananda Svarupa.*

Om or *Pranava* is a sparkling ferryboat for men who have fallen into the never-ending ocean of mundane life. Many have crossed this ocean of *Samsara* with the help .of this ferryboat. You can also do so if you will. Meditate constantly on Om with *bhava* and meaning and realise the Self.

Om is the ladder which takes the aspirant to the loftier levels of super-consciousness and spiritual heights of splendour and glory. Meditation on Om will reveal to you the laws of the higher planes and the spiritual laws. Meditation on Om will give you liberation, immortality, courage, inner spiritual strength, supreme peace, penetrative insight, and change your very being. It will transmute you into a *Jivanmukta*, a liberated sage.

You already know that radio waves travel in a second, seven times throughout the whole world. Mysterious indeed! Have you ever thought of this? Have you ever thought of the efficacy of this mysterious chanting of Om vibrations? If this scientific fact be true, what I believe is, that the vibrations of Om chanting have travelled throughout the world. From my experiences, personal and true, I boldly assert that it has brought solace, peace, full rest and cure to people suffering from appendicular colic in the Guy's and Bartholomew's Hospital of London. It has given immense relief to the ladies in the Maternity Hospital in the famous Rotunda, Dublin. These vibrations have again brought solace and comfort to the lepers in the hospitals of Dehra Dun, Chengelpet and Madras. It has soothed the nerves of the convalescents of the world. It has comforted thousands of virgin widows all over Bengal and Madras. It has brought solace to those depressed, sad persons, filled with gloom and despair. It has given strength to many unselfish workers in the world. It has infused a new spiritual life and vigour and vitality in the very hearts of enthusiastic youths, the future hope of India, a glory and blessing to the world at large. It has a great deal changed the vicious *Samskaras* that are imbedded in the subconscious mind, and the *Karanasarira*, the seed body of one and all. These are all true facts. Believe me sincerely, my amiable comrades! Have strong faith in my statement. Are you all ready now for recharging today? Siva will fill your heart again and again with the vibration of Om-chanting.

When a sacrificial rite or the like is found defective it will be rendered perfect by the utterance of this powerful Mantra Om in the end. With Om all acts of sacrifices, study of sacred scriptures, spiritual discipline and meditation are commenced. If the doer of sacrifices remembers Om, all obstacles that stand in the way of success of the sacrifices, are removed.

What does Lord Krishna teach by holding the flute in His hands? What is the symbolic philosophy of the flute? Flute is the symbol of Om. He says: "Empty your egoism. I will play in your body-flute. You will become one with My Will. Take refuge in Om. Meditate on Om. You will enter into My Being. Hear the inner soul-stirring music of the soul, music of Om, and rest in everlasting Peace."

Brahman is compared to the bird Hamsa. An adept in Yoga who bestrides the Hamsa i.e., contemplates on Om is not affected by Karmic influences or even by tens of crores of sins. Whoever does Japa of this Mantra in the morning destroys the sins committed during the day. Whosoever recites Om morning and evening becomes free from the sins, however sinful he may be, derives the good effects of the recitation of all the Vedas, and is freed from all the five great sins also. Such is the greatness and glory of Om, the name or symbol of Brahman. If you put unshakable faith in the glory of this name you will be freed from the bondage of births and deaths. If you perform any action with the utterance of Om in the beginning, middle and end, you will attain perfection and success in the action.

WHAT IS OM?

Om is the all-pervading sound that has come out of God. Om sound is the beginning of creation. Om has emanated from the cosmic vibration. Om is all in all. Om is the mystic word of power. Om is the magic word of marvellous potency. Om is the comforter and prop of all.

Just as the President represents the voice of the people of a country, so also Om represents the voice of all names of God, because Om is the substratum or the matrix or the basis of all sounds or names. In Om all names or sounds or words are included. Om is the king of all sounds or words. Om is the ocean into which all rivers of sounds, names and words flow.

Om is the voice of all creation. Om is Guru's voice. Om is the voice of *Hiranyagarbha*. Om is the voice of the Vedas. Om is the basis of all sounds. Om is the cosmic sound. Om is the primal sound of the universe. Om is the priceless treasure of a student in the path of *Jnana Yoga*. Om is the password of Vedantins. Om is the passport of those who are sailing in the boat of knowledge of the Self to reach the other shore of fearlessness and Immortality, Brahman.

Om is the Soul of souls. Om is the Light of lights. Om is the panacea for the destruction of sins and the dire disease of death. Om is the celestial ambrosia that confers immortality. Om is the sacred *Triveni* in the *Trikuti*. Meditate on Om. Plunge in Om. Have a dip in Om. This is the most sacred bath that will quench the fire of *Samsara*.

Om represents the canvas or the background. The forms of this universe represent the pictures in the canvas. The canvas is real, but the picture in the canvas is unreal, because fire in the canvas cannot burn your fingers, the knife in the canvas cannot cut your fingers, the tiger in the canvas cannot bite you. Even so, Om or Brahman is the only solid reality. The names and forms are unreal like the pictures in the canvas.

Om, the real Atman is the substratum for all the sounds, languages, body, mind, Prana and senses, the *Karana-sarira* and the five sheaths, and this universe. Just as the substratum is an under stratum or layer, a fundamental element, the substance in which qualities exist, so also Om is the substratum or the underlying reality in which all objects appear as waves in the ocean. The waves are mere appearances. So also the forms are mere appearances. The forms are unreal. Forms are unreal in the sense that they are only relatively real, that they are changing and impermanent. In the example of the ocean and wave, the ocean alone is real. Even so, Om or Brahman alone is real.

Om is a single syllable and of the nature of the Atman, all words are simplified into the one Pranava, the Om to describe Brahman. Om is Taraka Mantra i.e., the Mantra that helps man to cross the ocean of *Samsara*, the mundane existence. Taraka is Brahman alone. Taraka or Om alone should be worshipped.

Om is the essence of Vedanta. Om is the highest flower of the tree of Upanishads. Om is the root of the entire universe. Om is Akshara-Brahman. Om is the source of all words, articulations and languages. Om is the real name of Brahman. Om is the symbolic representation of Brahman, the Immortal-Self. Om is the word of power. Om is the Pranava. Om is the sacred monosyllable of the Vedas. Om is Udgita. Each of the component letters of Om is a symbol of each of the aspect in which Brahman is known.

Om is the spirit, substratum or essence. Om is the Immortal Soul. Om is the Holy Ghost. Om is the inner music of the Soul. Om is the music of the Silence. Om is the cream of Upanishads. Om is the supreme pinnacle of the magnificent hill of Vedanta.

That wherein there is neither hunger nor thirst, neither sorrow nor pain, neither 'you' nor 'he,' neither 'this' nor 'that,' neither 'here' nor 'there,' neither yesterday nor tomorrow, neither east nor west, neither sound nor colour, neither light nor darkness, neither seer nor seen, is Om.

That imperishable Brahmic seat or ineffable splendour, that indefinable, inexhaustible, illimitable Essence which pervades the whole universe, that which is called the continuum or the residuum or the noumenon by the Western Philosophers, that place where all speech stops, all thoughts cease, where the function of the intellect and all organs stop, is Om.

"Om is this;" "Om is the support;" "One with the pure desires should concentrate his mind upon the Atman through Om which is the Atman;" "Om is Brahman;" "The word Om is all"—these and a number of other texts of the Srutis clearly point out the usefulness of Om in the process of realising Brahman, the Immortal Self. They declare that Om, Brahman and the Atman are one and the same.

Om is the symbol and natural name of Brahman. Chanting of Om, *japa* of Om, singing of Om and meditation on Om, purify the mind, remove the tossing of the mind, destroy the veil of ignorance and help the aspirant to merge in Brahman.

All Mantras begin with Om. All Upanishads begin with Om. All religious ideas are centred in Om. The breath sings always Om, the song of infinity and Immortality. Thought of Om elevates the minds of all. The Christians, the Hebrews end their prayers with 'Amen' which is a modification of Om. The Muslims end their prayers with "Ahmeen," also a modification of Om. The Mandukya Upanishad, Mundaka Upanishad, Chhandogya Upanishad, Prasnopanishad,

Kathopanishad, the Gita and Brahma Sutras sing the glory of Om. Om is your very life. Om is your very breath. Om is the life of the Vedas. Om is the life of all Mantras. Om is the basis of this world. Om is everything. Om is a common Mantra. Om is the common property of all. All the various significances are centred in Om. Even Parvati and Sarasvati were not able to expound the significance of Om at full length. Such is the glory of Om. Om represents the Deity or the Soul of all religions and faiths, cults and schools. It should be accepted by everyone.

Just as the rope is the substratum of the snake and just as Brahman is the substratum of *prana*, mind, senses and the body, so also Om is the substratum or cause of the whole of the illusion of speech. The Sruti declares: "All is mere play of words;" "All is held together throughout by the string of speech or the cord of specific names;" "All is rendered possible in experience only by words." Nothing can exist apart from words. Names and forms are inseparable. Thought and language are inseparable. All effects are nothing but mere names. This whole phenomenal world of experience can never exist without names. All objects are necessarily to be named. You have to call a man by his name. Although there is nothing but Brahman, you cannot say 'Brahman,' 'Brahman,' 'Brahman,' 'Brahman,' when you wish to say "O Govind! give me water." Names cannot exist apart from Om. Therefore all is Om.

COMPOSITION OF OM

'A,' 'U,' 'M' are the life of all articulate words. 'A' and 'U' when connected together coalesce into 'O.' Therefore the right way to write Om, is 'AUM.' 'A' of the sacred monosyllable AUM is a symbol of the Virat aspect (gross manifestation), 'U' of Hiranyagarbha, Karya-brahman (subtle manifestation) and 'M' of the Isvara aspect, Karana-brahman, (unmanifested state of Brahman). Om is called the Sat-Nam or (EK) Omkara by the Sikhs, Jehovah by the Jews, Allah Hoo by the Muslims, Ahuramazda by Zoroastrians, Hanovn by the Persians, Elohem by the Christians, Tao by Chinese, and Monad by the Greeks. Om is called Pranava, because it runs through *prana* or the vital force and pervades life.

As already stated Om is split into 'A,' 'U' and 'M.' 'A' signifies the waking state (Jagrat Avastha), 'U' the dreaming state (Svapna Avastha) and 'M' the deep sleep state (Sushupti Avastha), while the Om taken as a single unit, stands for the fourth state, Turiya which transcends the above three states. The hypnotic rhythm of repetition of Om causes stillness in the mind. Chanting of Om, silent *japa* of Om and meditation on Om set up harmonious vibrations in the mind or subtle body, elevate the mind to magnanimous heights of divine splendour and eventually raise the consciousness to the state of Turiya wherein the meditator loses his individual consciousness and merges himself into the Supreme Soul, the all-pervading Brahmic Consciousness.

That which is Om is the imperishable, immutable noumenon, the Supreme Brahman. Om includes the experiences of man in the three states, viz., waking state, dreaming state and deep sleep state. Om stands for all the manifested and unmanifested planes. 'A' represents the physical plane and the waking state, 'U' represents the astral or mental plane and the dreaming state, 'M' indicates all that is beyond the reach of intellect, all that are unknown and the deep sleep state.

Corresponding to the four states, waking state, dreaming state, deep sleep state and *Turiya*, the mystic expression of Om is supposed to have four syllables, each representing a corresponding position of both in the macrocosm and microcosm.

The four sounds are 'A,' 'U,' 'M' and the indescribable vibration which is the essence of the whole (Ardhamatra). Now the purport of the Mandukya Upanishad which deals with this subject is to make the aspirant for Moksha, contemplate on the identity of 'A,' *Visva* and *Virat*; 'U,' Taijasa and

Hiranyagarbha; 'M' *Prajna* and Isvara; and the *Ardhamatra*, the essential vibration of Om, Turiya and the Pure Brahman. All these measures are devised in order that aspirant might grasp the highest Principle which transcends all mundane character. The universal aspects of Brahman which possess divine powers are, therefore, represented as one with the corresponding aspects in the individual. The Anandamaya state of the individual soul is looked upon as one with the Isvara state or universal soul.

'A' is Brahman, 'M' is *Maya* and 'U' is the interaction between the two 'A' and 'M.' The letters 'A' and 'U' are the two wings of the bird *Hamsa* (Om) of the form of Vishnu which goes to *Svarga*, the abode of Surya, the thousand-rayed God. The syllable Om bears in its heart all the Devas of the *Sattva-guna*. The syllable 'A' is considered to be its (the bird Om's) right wing, 'U' its left, 'M' its tail, and the Ardhamatra its head. From the letter 'A' came Brahma named Jambavan. From the letter 'U' came Upendra named Hari. From the letter 'M' came Siva known as Hanuman. Om also represents Tat-tvam-asi Mahavakya. 'A' is Jiva, 'M' is Isvara, and 'U' connects the two and shows the identity of Jiva and Isvara (Brahman).

In AUM, the letter 'A' stands for the masculine principle the Father; the letter 'U' stands for the female principle, the Mother; and the letter 'M' stands for the Son. It may also be said that 'A' stands for 'I,' 'U' for 'This' and 'M' for 'not.' So Om would mean 'I this not' *aham etat na*. It means neither 'I' nor 'this' nor 'not.' It signifies the one Self beyond names and forms, That which is, was and will be for ever.

Om is of eight limbs. 'A' is the first letter; 'U' is the second; 'M' is the third; Bindu is the fourth; Nada is the fifth; Kala is the sixth; Kalatita (that which is beyond Kala) is the seventh; and that which is beyond all these is the eighth. Akara, Ukara, Makara, Ardhamatra, Nada, Bindu, Kala and Sakti are the eight limbs of Om, Pranava.

Om is both *Saguna and Nirguna, Sakara* and *Nirakara.*
All triplets are represented by Om. Therefore Om is very important. It should be chanted and repeated mentally.

A	U	M
Brahma	Vishnu	Siva
Virat	Hiranyagarbha	Isvara
Visva	Taijasa	Prajna
Father	Son	Holy Ghost
Sarasvati	Lakshmi	Durga
Rajas	Sattva	Tamas
Body	Mind	Soul
Gross	Subtle	Causal
Jagrat	Svapna	Sushupti
Past	Present	Future
Sat	Chit	Ananda
Omniscience	Omnipotence	Omnipresence
Creation	Preservation	Destruction
Being	Becoming	Non-being
Sleep	Not sleep	Negation of the two
Prakriti	Jivatma	Paramatma
Birth	Life	Death

Here is an extract from Sri Rama Gita translated into
English by Pundit G. Krishna Sastri: "It is impossible to make
the average reader understand the occult significance and
the meaning attached to the names of these Mantras. They
refer to highly occult matters reserved for the last stages of
initiation. Those fortunate souls that have undergone the
highest states of initiation into the secrets of ancient Indian
white magic and occultism may, with advantage, refer to that
portion of "Vairavas Rahasya" which treats of Hrim and its six-

teen as well as the two hundred and fifty-six Matras. Hrim is said to be the Sthula-pranava and AUM the Sukshma-pranava.

The 256 Matras of this Pranava with their application are fully dealt within the "Anubhuti Mimamsa Bhashya" of Appaya Dikshitacharya.

The Mandukya Upanishad speaks of the Pranava as made up of 'A,' 'U,' 'M' and Ardhamatra. These when applied to Prakriti and Purusha become eight. Another Upanishad makes it sixteen and then thirty-two. The numbers 128 and then 256 give the further sub divisions of the Pranava. Of these, the first 96 refer to the Tattvas made up of the five vital currents, the five organs of knowledge and action, the five Pranas, mind, intelligence, the five Mahabhutas, the three states of consciousness, the six enemies of man (passions), the seven constituents of the body such as skin, blood, etc., the three Gunas (Sattva, Rajas and Tamas) and so on.

The primary meaning of Pranava is the Supreme One which is known to be of the nature of undivided Existence-knowledge-bliss Absolute (Sat-chit-ananda). This enables man to get over to the other shore of the ocean of Samsara. Of the 256 Matras, 128 pertain to the Saguna-brahman and 128 to the Nirguna-brahman. The 128 Matras of the Saguna-brahman demonstrate the Svagatabheda. This is illustrated by the difference existing between the root, branches, leaves, fruits, etc., of the one and the same tree. The tree is the same, but still there are differences between the different parts like branch, leaves, etc. This is said to be the difference among the several members in the body. 16 of these 128 Matras go to make up the 16 sub divisionals into the gross, the subtle, etc., of the four characteristics known by the names of Viveka, Vairagya, Shad-sampat and Mumukshutva. These pertain to the 16 Atmadhikarins or persons fit for realising the Self. These states are Sthulaviveka, Sukshmaviveka, Karanaviveka, Turiyaviveka, etc. The remaining 112 are distributed among

the seven Jnana Bhumikas. The meditation on this Pranava
in the form of muttered prayer is useful for attaining
Krama-mukti (progressive emancipation). This is subordi-
nate. But the abstract meditation on this is the best. The
meanings of other names used by devotees are included in
the meaning of Pranava.

SIXTEEN STATES OF CONSCIOUSNESS

There are sixteen states of consciousness. They are
made up as follows: There are the four primary states of consciousness called *Jagrat, Svapna, Sushupti* and *Turiya.*
These by differentiation multiply into sixteen. These are
Jagrat-jagrat, (waking in waking), Jagrat-Svapna (waking in
dreaming), Jagrat-sushupti (waking in sleep), Jagrat-turiya
(waking in Turiya) and so on, with the remaining three other
primary consciousnesses.

That is called Jagrat-jagrat state in which there are no
such ideas as 'this' or 'mine' regarding all visible things. The
great ones call that state Jagrat-svapna in which all ideas of
name and form are given up. This is preceded by the realisation of the nature of Sat-chit-ananda. In the state of
Jagrat-sushupti there is no idea except Self-knowledge. In
Jagrat-turiya, the conviction is firm that the three states,
gross, subtle and causal are false. In Svapna-jagrat there comes the conviction that even the activities proceeding from
the astral plane owing to cause set in motion previously, do
not bind the self when the knowledge of the physical plane is
destroyed. In Svapna there is seer, seen and sight. When the
Karana-ajnana (ignorance, the root of all) is destroyed, it is
Svapna-sushupti where by means of excessive subtle thinking, the modifications of one's own mind become merged in
knowledge. That is Svapna-turiya in which the innate bliss
(pertaining to the individual self) is lost by the attainment of
universal bliss. That state is called Sushupti-jagrat in which
the experience of self-bliss takes the shape of Universal
Intelligence through the rising of mental modifications. In

Sushupti-svapna one identifies himself with the modifications of the mind which has long been immersed in the experience of internal bliss. When one attains oneness of knowledge (Bodhaikata) which is above these mental modifications and above the realisation of the abstract condition of the Lord, he is said to be in Sushupti-sushupti in Sushupti-turiya, Akhandaikarasa the one Undivided Essence manifests of its own accord. When the enjoyment of the above said Akhandaikarasa is natural in the waking state, one is said to be in Turiya-jagrat. Turiya-svapna is difficult to be attained. It is a state in which the enjoyment of Akhandaikarasa becomes natural even in his dreaming condition. The higher state of Turiya-sushupti is still more difficult to be accomplished. In this state even in deep sleep Akhandaikarasa clearly manifests itself to the Yogi. The highest stage is Turiya-turiya wherein Akhandaikarasa disappears like the dust of Kataka nut (the nut of *strychnos potatorum*, used for clearing water). This stage is the Arupa one and is beyond cognisance. These sixteen states are difficult to be accomplished in one birth. Still they are to be attempted. The sixteen parts are Matras of Om are said to be the form of the Universal Brahmic Consciousness. They represent the above mentioned sixteen grades of consciousness. The remaining 112 (out of 128) are only subdivisions of the seven Bhumikas and represent the various states of these sixteen. Here the 128 Matras are those pertaining to the Nirguna and not to the Saguna aspect.

CHAPTER II

MEDITATION ON OM

SADHANA

Om is your best companion in life because it gives you Immortality and eternal Bliss. Om is your Sadguru. Om is your guide and preceptor. Therefore, keep company or constant Satsanga with Om by practising Japa of Om, chanting of Om, Smarana of Om, Chintana of Om, Manana of Om, Vichara of Om, meditation of Om.

Japa of Om is constant repetition of Om either verbally, mentally or in a humming manner. Chanting of Om is loud repetition and taking the breath and vibrations from the Muladhara Chakra to Sahasrara Chakra. Smarana of Om is remembrance of Om or Brahman. *Chintana* of Om is thinking of Om. Manana is reflection of Om. *Vichara* of Om is enquiry into the nature of Brahman. Meditation of Om is Nididhyasana on the invisible, immortal Self with Advaita Bhava or feeling: "I am the all-pervading Brahman, the pure Consciousness." This feeling should go deep into the very core of your heart. Every cell, every pore of your body, every atom, every molecule, every nerve, every fibre, every drop of blood, every artery, every vein should powerfully vibrate or pulsate, with this sacred, soul-elevating, sublime feeling. When you chant Om or meditate on Om or sing Om feel that you are one with the supreme Self. Transcend the world of names and forms and identify yourself with the all-pervading pure Consciousness.

There are various ways in Nirguna meditation, viz., Laya Chintana of Om, Laya Chintana of Antahkarana (mind), Laya Chintana of elements, Anvayavyatireka method,

Neti-neti method (I am not the body; I am not the mind; I am Sat-chit-ananda Brahman; I am Sakshi), Adhyaropa-apavada method, Bhaga-tyaga Lakshana method, repetition of Om with its meaning, etc. Some reach Brahman by transcending the Pancha-kosas; some through Avasthatraya Sakshi Bhava; some through the three Gunas (identifying with the Trigunatita Ananda Brahman). Soham Dhyana is associated with breath. Here the mind is fixed on the breath.

JAPA OF OM

The *japa* of Om (Pranava Japa) has a tremendous influence on the mind. The pronunciation of the sacred word Om is one which has engaged the attention of all aspirants. The vibrations set up by the same word are so powerful that, if persisted in, they would bring the largest building to the ground. This seems difficult to believe until one has tried to practise, but once having tried it, one can easily understand how the above statement can be true and correct perfectly. I have tested the power of the vibrations and can quite believe that the effect would be as stated. Pronounced as spelt, it will have a certain effect upon the student, but pronounced in its correct method, it arouses and transforms every atom in his physical body, setting up new vibrations and conditions and awakening the spiritual power in the body.

As soon as you sit for meditation chant Om loudly for five minutes. This will remove Vikshepa or tossing of mind, shut out all worldly thoughts and generate sublime and soul-stirring thoughts. It will produce harmony in the five *kosas* or sheaths and keep you in tune with the Infinite. Then take to silent or mental *japa* of Om.

CHANTING OF OM

Chant Om from the very bottom of your heart with profound feeling. When chanting Om, knowing its omniscience, omnipotence and omnipresence, feel that Om gushes forth with its true colour, from every nerve, every vein, every cell, every atom, every molecule, every electron and the very blood corpuscle of your body. Pour forth Om vibrations into the world with mighty vigour, speed, force and strength. Get ready now for recharging. Now roar like a lion of Vedanta and chant Om.

Chant Om for five minutes rhythmically with *bhava* and understanding as soon as you sit for meditation. Learn its meaning. The sound should start from the navel and end at the crown of the head. The mysterious vibrations produced by the chanting of Om will produce one-pointedness of mind and harmony in the Annamaya, Pranamaya and Manomaya Kosas (food sheath, vital sheath and mental sheath) and make the mind in tune with the Infinite.

Drive evil thoughts by chanting Om. Draw inspiration, power and strength by singing Om. Get one-pointedness of mind by doing Japa of Om. Melt the mind in Brahman by meditating on Om and rest in your own Sat-chit-ananda Svarupa. May that Om guide you, protect you, elevate you, take you to the goal and free you from the round of births and deaths.

Whenever you feel depressed, whenever you get a little headache, take a brisk walk and chant Om while walking. While chanting Om feel that your entire being is filled with divine energy. Chanting of Om is a potent, easily available tonic and specific for all diseases. Om is a panacea or sovereign remedy for all ailments. Try this prescription yourself and feel the miraculous effects of this divine medicine. Just as you take medicine twice or thrice, take recourse of chanting of Om twice or thrice. Brahman, the Atman, is one with Om. Chanting of Om means going near to the source and tapping the cosmic energy which is inexhaustible. When you chant Om feel: 'All health I am.' All pathogenic or disease causing germs are destroyed or burnt by the vibrations of Om. You can chant Om while sitting on any comfortable Asana in your room for the purpose of regaining, maintaining or improving your health.

OM WITH PRANAYAMA

You can associate Om with the breath during the practice of Pranayama. Mentally repeat 'O' during inhalation and 'M' during exhalation. This will increase the efficacy of Pranayama. This is Sagarbha pranayama. You can keep Om for constant Ajapa-japa also. Watch the breath and repeat 'O' during inspiration and 'M' during expiration. You can do this practice while walking also. Put sufficient force into the thoughts of Om. Feel that Om is coming from your Soul. This will raise your consciousness to a very high plane. You will become one with the Soul, the Atman.

Meditate that the single letter, the supreme light, the Pranava, Om is the origin or source of these three letters 'A,' 'U' and 'M.' Inhale the air through the left nostril for the space of 16 Matras, meditate on the letter 'A' during that time, retain the air for the space of 64 Matras, meditate on the letter 'U' during the time, exhale for the space of 32 Matras and meditate on the letter 'M' during that time. Practise this again and again in the above order. Begin with 2 or 3 times and gradually increase the number to 20 or 30 times according to your capacity and strength. To begin with, keep the ratio 1:4:2. Gradually increase the ratio to 16:64:32. The practitioner will get great peace of mind and inner strength. Kundalini will be awakened. He will soon enter into Nirvikalpa Samadhi.

YUKTI

There are many illustrations and Yuktis in Vedanta. Each student should take up that illustration that suits his taste and temperament, and that makes the mind more inward to rest in his Atman. Sometimes various kinds of doubts such as 'whether God exists,' 'whether I am really the Atman' and wrong conceptions such as 'I am the body,' 'world is real' attack the student and produce distraction of the mind. Through *yukti* and *drishtanta* he should drive them at once and try to rest in his *svarupa*.

The illustration of crystal and blue cloth or red flower will remove the Kartritva Bhranti, the delusion 'I am the actor.' The illustration of reflection in the sun will remove the Bheda-bhranti, delusion of difference. The illustration of pot-space will remove Sanga-bhranti, the delusion of attachment. The illustration of snake in the rope will obviate the Vikarabhranti, the delusion of modification. The illustration of gold and ornament will remove the Jagat Satya Bhranti, the delusion of the reality of the world. The illustration of bubbles, foam, waves and ocean, blueness in the sky, mirage in the sand, magnet and iron, iron ball and fire, sun and its rays, mud and pots, thread and cloth, silver in the mother-of-pearl, will help the student to remove some of his other doubts. If you remember these illustrations occasionally, many of your doubts will be cleared. The idea of Brahman will be strengthened.

TRATAKA ON OM

Neophytes in the path of Jnana Yoga should do Trataka (gazing) on Om with open eyes in the beginning for about three months. Then they should visualise Om with closed eyes. Visualisation of Om is the calling up of a clear mental image of Om by closing the eyes. They should repeat Om mentally with feeling and meaning and make the ears hear the sound also so that they may not run outside to hear other sounds.

Have the picture of Om in front of you in your meditation room. Concentrate on this picture. Do Trataka also with open eyes. Steady gazing without winking make tears flow profusely. Associate the ideas of infinity, eternity, immortality, etc., when you think of Om. This is meditation with and without attributes. Keep a picture of Om always before your mind and do worship. Burn incense, camphor. Offer flowers. This is suitable for modern educated people. This is a combined method of *bhakti* and *jnana*.

MEDITATION ON OM

Meditation on Om with feeling and meaning leads to realisation of Self. This is the Vedantic Sadhana. This is Jnana Yoga.

Meditation is the keeping up of the continuous flow of one idea of Brahman in the mind like the flow of oil from one vessel to another vessel (*Taila dhara-vat*).

When you chant or sing Om, melt the mind in the Immortal Self and feel that you are the Light of lights, the Lord of lords, Emperor of emperors, King of kings, the Soul of souls, the Self of all selves, the Eye of all eyes, the Ear of all ears, the Prana of all Pranas, the Director or Governor of this world, the Immortal Brahman of the Upanishads of whom the Sama chanters sing with the Vedas and the Angas in the *pada* and *krama* methods, of whom the Rishis and sages have sung in manifold ways in many various chants and in decisive, Brahma-sutra words, full of reasonings.

Deny the body. Deny the world. Assert '*Aham Brahma Asmi*.' Be established on the one idea "*Ahamatma*—I am the Self," "*Aham Chaitanya*—I am Consciousness." Do not bleat like a lamb. Do not think 'I am the body,' 'I am so and so,' 'I am Mr. Peter, John, David or Pantulu or Prasad.' Dehypnotise yourself now. You are the real Supreme Self, Sat-chit-ananda Atman.

Whenever the ideas of the world and body get stronger in your mind, remember the two Vadas, Vivarta-vada and Drishthi-srishti-vada. At once these ideas will be thinned out and you will proceed further in meditation. The analogy of snake in the rope, is Vivarta-vada. Whenever you begin to see, the world appears, the world is a mental projection only. There is no Srishti. This is Drishthi-srishti-vada.

Enter the ship of Om. Start the propeller, the current of Brahma-bhavana, I am Brahman, I am the immortal, all-pervading Self. Sail smoothly in the ocean of Samsara with the help of constant meditation. Put the anchor of discrimination. Whenever the tempest of Vasanas blows vehemently, get ready to wear the lifebelt of Atma-vichara, the enquiry of the Self; whenever there is the fear of the ship being shattered by the iceberg of worldly infatuation, land safely in the marvellous city of Sat-chit-ananda-brahman.

When your Advaita-nishtha is accompanied by the utterance of Aham Brahma Asmi, you get Sabdanuvida Savikalpa Samadhi. When the repetition drops down, you enter into the pure Nirvikalpa Avastha.

Para-vairagya is Antaranga Sadhana for entering into Nirvikalpa Samadhi. All the objects appear as Atyanta Mithya like mirage in the sand. Even all subtle desires will entirely vanish, when you develop this type of highest Vairagya.

When you attain the Nirvikalpa Samadhi, the meditation drops. The meditator and the meditated become identical. The thinker and the thought become one. There is Triputilaya, dissolution of the triad—knower, knowledge and knowable.

He who meditates on Om becomes a spiritual dynamo. He radiates joy, peace and power to those who come in contact with him. He fills the world with spiritual vibrations. He becomes a channel for the inflow of spiritual force or divine energy. He knows the relationship between the universe and man, between man and man, between man and Brahman. He beholds the Self in all beings and all beings in the Self eventually. The whole mystery of creation and the riddle of this universe are revealed unto him like Amalaka fruit in the hand. He becomes a spiritual hero in the Adhyatmic battlefield who has won the laurels of knowledge of Self by gaining victory over the mind and senses, the enemies of knowledge and peace.

The goal can only be attained through the Dhyana on this mystic symbol Om. Meditation on Om is the only real, royal road to the attainment of salvation. Meditation kills all pains, sufferings and sorrows. Meditation destroys all causes of sorrow. Meditation gives vision of unity. Meditation induces sense of oneness. Meditation is a balloon or parachute or the aeroplane that helps the aspirant to soar high into the realms of eternal bliss, everlasting peace and undying joy.

It is to attain the different Samadhis that this Pranava is useful. As the letter 'Ham' represents the Self which is devoid of egoism (Aham) and the letter 'Sah' denotes its identity with Brahman, this word 'Hamsah' itself teaches the direct identity of the Self and Brahman. One who has realised this is a Paramahamsa. The Sannyasins are ordained to meditate on the Pranava for this very reason. They have already reached a high stage and meditation on Om raises them further and ultimately they become Paramahamsas.

O spotless Vivek! O taintless Prakas! O deathless Amara! Thou art Om. Thou art Divinity of divinities, Deva of Devas. *Maya* is your illusive power. Thou art the Lord of *maya*. All nature will pay tribute to you when you rest in Om. The Himalayas, the sun, the moon and stars, the vast sky and the ocean, proclaim your ineffable glory. All mighty rivers, the manifold forms, various kinds of beautiful flowers, etc., declare thy splendour and brilliance. Rest in Om. Live in Om. Become that Om. Om is thy sweet immortal abode, the original home of indescribable effulgence or lustre.

SAGUNA AND NIRGUNA MEDITATION

Have the picture of Om in front of you. Concentrate on it. Do Trataka also with open eyes (steady gazing without winking till tears flow profusely). This is both Saguna and Nirguna meditation.

Meditation on a concrete object or on the Murty of Lord Rama or Lord Krishna or Lord Siva is Saguna (Sakara) meditation or Sthula Dhyana (concrete meditation with form or attributes). Meditation on Om, Soham, Sivoham or Mahavakyas (A*ham Brahma Asmi* or *Tat Tvam Asi*) is

Nirguna-nirakara meditation or Sukshma-dhyana or abstract formless, attributeless meditation. Vedantins use the term Nididhyasana, for meditation. Meditation on Om with Brahma-bhavana is Ahamgraha Upasana.

Those who have subtle intellect, bold understanding, strong will, courage and self-reliance alone are qualified persons for this type of meditation. Those who have purity of heart, One-pointedness of mind, the four means of salvation (Sadhana Chatushtaya), Yukti and ability are fit to take up this meditation. Meditation on Soham is also Nirguna meditation. Nirguna meditation is Vedantic Sadhana. It is the practice of Jnana Yoga. Brahma-chintana, Brahma-abhyasa, Jnana-abhyasa, Abheda-chintana, Pranava-upasana, Tattva-abhyasa are synonymous terms for Nirguna meditation. Those who have done concrete meditation for some months or years can take to Nirguna meditation easily. Those who jump at once to Nirguna meditation will experience some difficulty.

Even in Nirguna meditation there is abstract image in the beginning. Meditation on ice and its qualities is concrete meditation. Meditation on steam is abstract meditation. Meditate on the physical form of your father. This is one form of concrete (Saguna) meditation. Meditate on the qualities of your father. This is abstract meditation. Meditate on a green leaf. This is one kind of concrete meditation. Meditate on greenness. This is abstract meditation. Meditate on the void. Meditate on the blue sky. Meditate on the all-pervading light of the sun. Imagine that there is infinite ocean of light. Meditate on the formless air or all-pervading ether. These are all types of Nirguna meditation. These preliminary practices will make the mind more and more subtle and render it fit to take up Vedantic Nididhyasana.

Meditate on Om as silence, an embodiment of peace. This is abstract or subtle meditation (Sukshma Dhyana). Meditate on Om with the feeling: "I am an embodiment of Silence or Peace." This is Vedantic Nirguna meditation or

Ahamgraha Upasana. Meditate on Om as an embodiment of bliss or Ananda. This is also abstract meditation. Meditate on Om with the Bhava: "I am an embodiment of Bliss." This is Ahamgraha Upasana. Do you see clearly the difference between the two forms of meditation now? The first kind of meditation will prepare you for the practice of the second kind of meditation.

Nirguna means without attributes. It does not mean that Brahman is a perfect void. It means that there are Ananta Kalyana Gunas in Brahman. It means that there are no such perishable qualities, as the blue colour of a cloth, etc., in Brahman. Further there is no Guna or Guni in Brahman. Brahman is embodiment of infinite divine Gunas. This is the significance of the term 'Nirguna.' Brahman is Bliss itself. Brahman is Knowledge itself. Brahman is Beauty itself. Brahman is Light itself.

Try to become one with the sound in the beginning when you meditate on Om or repeat Om mentally. As you advance in your practice you should entertain the feeling: "I am all-pervading pure Sat-chit-ananda Atman." You need not be one with the sound now. What is wanted is feeling with the meaning of 'I am Brahman.'

May the Divine Flame grow brighter in you all! May the Divine Light lighten the spiritual path! May Divine Glory shine on you for ever! May peace and harmony fill your hearts, minds and the cells of your very being!

LAYA CHINTANA OF OM

Laya Chintana of Om leads to Advaita Nishtha or Nirvikalpa Samadhi:

(a) Visva gets Laya (dissolution) in Virat; Virat in 'A.'

(b) Taijasa gets Laya in Hiranyagarbha; Hiranyagarbha in 'U.'

(c) Prajna gets Laya in Isvara; Isvara in 'M.'

(d) Turiya is common to both Jiva and Isvara. Amatra gets Laya in Brahman (Kutastha-brahma-aikyam), oneness of Jiva and Brahman.

This is Laya Chintana of AUM. This is very useful for meditation on Om.

CHAPTER III

FORMULAE FOR MEDITATION

Meditate on Om. Retire into your meditation chamber. Sit on Padma, Siddha or Sukhasana. Close your eyes, relax the muscles and nerves completely. Concentrate the gaze on Trikuti, the space between the two eyebrows. Silence the objective or conscious mind. Repeat Om mentally with Brahma-bhavana. This Bhavana is a *sine qua non*. You will have to repeat Om with the feeling that you are the infinite, all-pervading pure intelligence. Repeat the following formulae mentally with feeling. Renounce the idea that you are different from Brahman. Practise regularly, steadily with interest, faith, zeal, perseverance and enthusiasm. Have congenial company and light Sattvic food. Practise for three hours in the morning from 4 a.m. and for 3 hours at night. Keep up the Brahmic feeling while at work also. You are bound to succeed.

I

All-pervading, ocean of light I am	Om Om Om
Light of lights I am	Om Om Om
Sun of suns I am	Om Om Om
Infinity I am	Om Om Om
Pure Chit (consciousness) I am	Om Om Om
All-pervading infinite Light I am	Om Om Om
Vyapaka, Paripurna, Jyotirmaya Brahman I am	Om Om Om
Omnipotent, Omniscient I am	Om Om Om

All-bliss, all-purity, all-glory I am	Om Om Om
All joy, all health I am	Om Om Om

II

Absolute is the only Reality	
(Brahma Satyam)	Om Om Om
Aham Brahmasmi	Om Om Om
I am all-pervading pure Consciousness	Om Om Om
I am the living Truth	Om Om Om
I am the living Reality	Om Om Om
Akhanda Ekarasa Chinmatroham (I am	
the one unbroken pure Consciousness	Om Om Om
Chinmayoham (I am mass of knowledge)	Om Om Om
Sat-chit-ananda Svarupoham	Om Om Om
Asangoham (I am unattached)	Om Om Om
Bhumananda Svarupoham	
(I am Infinity Bliss)	OM OM Om
Kevaloham (I am alone)	Om Om Om

III

Hamsa Soham—Soham Hamsa	Om Om Om
Nirmaloham (I am purity)	Om Om Om
Paripurnoham (I am all-full)	Om Om Om
Kuthasthoham, Aham Sakshi	
(I am Changeless, I am witness)	Om Om Om
Aham Chaitanya, Aham Atma	Om Om Om
Vimaloham, Amaloham	Om Om Om
Advaitoham, Asangoham	Om Om Om
Chinmatroham, Chaitanyoham	Om Om Om

Sivoham, Sivahkevaloham	Om Om Om
Paripurnoham, Paramatmoham	Om Om Om
Nitya Tripta Svarupoham	Om Om Om
Nishkaloham (I am partless)	Om Om Om
Nirgunoham (I am attributeless)	Om Om Om

IV

I am distinct from the three bodies (Sariratraya Vilakshana)	Om Om Om
I am distinct from five Kosas (Pancha-kosa Vyatirikta)	Om Om Om
I am witness of three states (Avasthatraya Sakshi)	Om Om Om
I am Sakshi, Drashta, Turiya	Om Om Om
I am embodiment of Turiya	Om Om Om
I am Akarta, Abhokta, Asanga Sakshi	Om Om Om

You can meditate on the above series of ideas. Finally you should allow the mind to settle on one idea only. Give up this idea also. Shut out all worldly ideas. Now Brahmakara Vritti will be raised. This will destroy the original Avidya, Mula Ajnana that covers the Brahman. You will shine in pristine Brahmic glory. You will realise your identity or oneness with the Supreme Self.

CHAPTER IV

BRAHMAKARA VRITTI

Brahman is Sat-chit-ananda (Existence Absolute, Knowledge Absolute, Bliss Absolute). He is Being, Consciousness, Bliss. He is the source of everything. In Him we live, move and have our very being. He is the source for the world and the Vedas. He is the substratum and essence of all these visible objects. He gives light and power to mind, intellect, Prana and the organs. He witnesses as Kutastha the motives and modifications that arise in the mind.

Mind is Brahma-sakti. Antahkarana is a Sanskrit term which means internal instrument. It is synonymous with the mind. It is used in a broad sense. It includes *manas, buddhi, chitta* and *ahamkara*. *Vritti* is a whirlpool. It is a wave of thought that arises on the surface of the lake-mind. This *vritti* is caused by the operation of psychic Prana on the mind. The highest manifestation of *prana* is *vritti* or thought and the lowest manifestation of *prana* is breathing. Innumerable Vrittis constantly emanate from the mind. A ray of the mind actually comes out through eyes and assumes the shape and form of the object and envelops it. It removes the veil termed Tula Avidya in Vedantic parlance that envelops all objects. This Vritti is styled as Vishayakara Vritti. The function of a Vritti is to cause Avarana Bhanga, removal of veil. A *vritti* of a pot removes the veil that envelops the pot and the pot becomes the object of perception. You then say: "This is a pot." This is the Vedantic theory of perception. I think you have a clear comprehensive understanding of what Vishayakara *vritti* is. Vishayas are objects of sense-enjoyment. *Akara* means form. The mind assumes the form of the object it sees. This is Vishayakara.

The Jiva or individual soul in a state of ignorance makes friendship with the mind and in unison with the mind, *vritti* and senses, enjoys the objects of this world daily. As soon as he joined with the mind, Vritti and the senses, he began to taste the 'forbidden fruit.' He degraded himself to a state of Jiva with passion and emotions. He was caught up in the Samsaric wheel of birth and death. This Vishayakara Vritti is constantly arising in the instinctive or gross mind which is filled with passions. This should be converted by spiritual Sadhana and constant Vichara into the pure Sattvic Brahmakara Vritti.

What is this Brahmakara Vritti? Wherefrom does it originate? How can we know that this Vritti has made its appearance? What are its Lakshanas? What is its function? What is its final fate? How can we generate this Vritti?

I shall deal at full length now on these salient points. This is an expanded Vritti that proceeds from Sattvic Antahkarana. When the mind is cleansed of its impurities such as passion, anger, covetousness, infatuation, pride, jealousy, hypocrisy, intolerance, egoism, attachment, hatred, laziness and torpidity, becomes Sattvic, pure and calm.

Mind contains three Doshas, faults, viz., Mala (impurities), Vikshepa (tossing) and Avarana (veil of ignorance). The Mala is removed by Upasana, worship of the tutelary deity. The senses should be controlled by the practice of Dama, self-restraint. The mind should be rendered calm by the practice of Sama through Vasana Tyaga. One should be equipped with the four means of salvation: (1) *viveka*, discrimination between the Real and the unreal; (2) *vairagya*, indifference to sense enjoyments; (3) *shadsampat*, sixfold virtues, viz., *sama* (peace of mind), *dama* (subjugation of the Indriyas), *titiksha* (power of endurance), *uparati* (satiety), *sraddha* (faith) and *samadhana* (one-pointed mind) and (4) *mumukshutva* (desire for salvation).

After equipping himself with these four qualifications, the aspirant should approach the Sadguru. He should hear the Srutis from him. The Sadguru will explain *in extenso* the nature of Advaita Brahman, the One secondless Existence. This is termed *sravana*. The Sadguru will explain the Lakshyartha (real indicative meaning) of Mahavakyas, great sentences of the Vedas such as *Tat-tvam-asi*, *Aham Brahmasmi,* etc. Through the Neti-neti doctrine, the Sadguru will negate the five Kosas, body, *prana*, Mind, *buddhi* and the causal body. The Sadguru will affirm: "O aspirant, you are up to this time affected by *avidya*, ignorance. You are not this physical body. You are not the *prana*. You are not the mind. You are not the *buddhi*. You are not the Anandamayakosa. You are different from the five sheaths. You are the Witness of the three states, waking, dreaming and deep sleep. You are the eternal, ever pure, ever free, all-pervading, all-full, one essence, Sat-chit-ananda Brahman, *Tat-tvam-asi—* Thou art That."

The aspirant will constantly reflect over this new, lofty Advaitic idea *Aham Brahmasmi*. This is termed Manana in Vedantic parlance. After Manana, he will practise Nididhyasana, on the one idea: *Aham Brahmasmi*. Now the Brahmakara Vritti is generated. Hear the words of Sri Sankaracharya in his reputed Atma Bodha. He gives a method to raise this expanded Vritti from the pure, Sattvic Antahkarana:

> *Evam nirantarabhyasta brahmaivasmiti vasana,*
> *Haratyavidya-vikshepan roganiva rasayanam.*

"Such incessant impression on the mind that 'I am verily Brahman' removes the turbulence of ignorance, as the elixir of life cures all diseases."

Now comes the actual Sadhana. Sitting in a lonely place with the mind freed from all passions, with the senses subjugated, one should contemplate on that one Infinite Self without thinking of anything else.

For Nididhyasana solitude is indispensable. It is a *sine qua non.* You can convert a solitary room into a forest. Or if circumstances can permit, preferably, you can have seclusion in Rishikesh or Uttarakashi (Himalayas) for three years. This Vedantic Nididhyasana is incessant contemplation of one idea *Aham Brahmasmi.* During contemplation on this one idea, the Brahmakara Vritti is generated. So Brahmakara Vritti is *Aham Brahmasmi Mahavakya Janya Sattvic Antahkarana Parinama*—a modification of the pure mind, born of meditation on the Mahavakya *Aham Brahmasmi.*

An aspirant equipped with Sadhana Chatushtaya and the real significance of *Aham Brahmasmi* Mahavakya can only generate the Brahmakara Vritti by practising constant, deep meditation on *Aham Brahmasmi,* dwelling in solitude without thinking of any worldly object. When this Brahmakara Vritti is in operation or manifestation, all Vishaya Vrittis vanish.

In the beginning of the Sadhana a fight goes on between Brahmakara Vritti and Vishayakara Vritti. As soon as the former Vritti manifests, the Vishayakara Vrittis try their level best to destroy the Brahmakara Vritti. Objective thoughts try to enter. They actually appear and also the Sadhaka comes down from Brahmakara Vritti to Vishayakara Vritti. Again he elevates himself to Brahmakara Vritti. By constant effort he is able to keep the Brahmakara Vritti for some time. All the Sankalpas stop.

As soon as the Brahmakara Vritti manifests, the Sadhaka has a few glimpses of Brahman. It is extremely difficult to keep up the Brahmakara Vritti for a long time. It is extremely difficult to have Brahmakara Vritti Sthiti permanently like the steady flow of oil. Swami Vishuddhananda had the glimpses only. But Sri Sankara and Dattatreya had Brahmakara Vritti Sthiti (Bhuma). Glimpses also do surely liberate a man from Samsara as the Vasanas are completely destroyed. A deep study of Nirvana Prakarana of Yoga Vasishtha will throw much light on this Brahmakara Vritti.

Other names for this Brahmakara Vritti are: Akhandakara Vritti, Tadakara Vritti, Atmakara Vritti, Svarupakara Vritti, Akhanda Ekarasa Vritti.

Advaita Bhavana Rupa Samadhi is Vritti Sahita, associated with Brahmakara Vritti. In Advaita Avasthanarupa Samadhi there is no Vritti. It is Vritti Rahita.

The mind becomes that on which it intensely meditates in accordance with the analogy of wasp and caterpillar (Bhramarakita Nyaya). By constantly meditating on Brahman, the purified mind becomes Brahman. This is termed Vritti Tadakara.

Just as the paste of *kataka* fruit when thrown in impure water carries down all its impurity and at the same time goes down itself to the bottom of the vessel, this Brahmakara Vritti destroys the primitive Ajnana or Mula-avidya that envelops the Svarupa and thereby this phenomenal world melts itself in Brahman. The function of this Brahmakara Vritti is to remove the *avarana* that envelops Brahman, and after this is done, it dies by itself, just as in the burial ground the long stick used in burning the dead body gets itself burnt up after burning up the dead body.

In the case of perception of an object, the Vishayakara Vritti removes the Avarana of Tula Avidya that envelops the object and the reflected intelligence (Abhasa Chaitanya or Vritti Sahita Chaitanya—intelligence associated with Vritti) makes the object clear. In the case of Brahmakara Vritti it is different. There is also intelligence that is associated with this Brahmakara Vritti. Suppose there is a small book inside a pot in a dark room. When the pot is broken you will not be able to see the book. You need the aid of a lamp. Suppose there is a small lamp inside the pot in the same dark room. When the pot is broken, the lamp shines by itself without the help of any extraneous light. So also when the *avarana* that envelops Brahman is removed by Brahmakara Vritti, Brahman shines by Himself in His own Glory as He is Self-luminous. The intelligence that accompanies the Brahmakara Vritti is not necessary to make Brahman appear. But in the case of perception of an object, the intelligence that is associated with the Vritti is necessary to make the object appear. This is the difference.

Brahmakara Vritti is only a means and not the end. In Brahman, there is no Vritti Jnana. In Brahman, there are no Vrittis; there is Svarupa Jnana. Brahman is Chidghana, a mass of Knowledge. All *vrittis* should be given up before Brahma Jnana is obtained. Even the one final Brahmakara Vritti should be merged.

You may ask why the term Brahmakara Vritti is given to the last explained Sattvic Vritti, when Brahman has no Akara. When all the Vishayakara Vrittis stop, then the Brahmakara Vritti comes out and this *vritti* is a means to approach Brahman. So it is correctly termed Brahmakara Vritti. Different kinds of formulae given in this book in Chapter III will help you to raise this Brahmakara Vritti through meditation.

Thousand thanks to the Brahmakara Vritti which helps us to reach the highest end of human existence. Thanks to *Tat-tvam-asi* and *Aham Brahmasmi* Mahavakyas also. Than gaining which there is no greater gain, than whose bliss there is no higher bliss, than which knowledge there is no higher knowledge—that should be understood as Svarupa or Brahman, Sat-chit-ananda. In essence, thou art Brahman; thou art Sat-chit-ananda Svarupa. Realise this by generating the Brahmakara Vritti and be free.

May you all generate the Brahmakara Vritti from the Sattvic Antahkarana, the pure intellect rendered sharp and subtle by Japa and meditation of Om, and practice of the fourfold *sadhana*. May you all realise this non-dual state of eternal bliss through meditation on Om. May you all enter into Advaita-nishtha or Nirvikalpa Samadhi which fries all worldly *samskaras* and *vasanas* and which bestows Immortality

through Pranava Upasana. May you all rest in your Sat-chit-
ananda Svarupa which is beyond the mind and speech,
through Brahma Bhavana!

CHAPTER V

SONGS AND KIRTANS ON OM

WHAT IS OM

(SONG)

What is Om?
Om is Sat, Om is Chit,
Om is Anand, Om is Vyapak,
Om is Atma, Om is Brahman,
Om Is Purusha, Om is Soul   That is Om.

What is Om?
Om is a fortress; Om is a place
Built to shut out hate and malice,
Built to shut in joy and love,
And a blessing from above,   That is Om.

What is Om?
Om is a house of treasure,
Pearls of knowledge, Bank of wisdom,
Gems of bliss, and Gold of grace,
Wisdom-nectar, Light of lights,   That is Om.

What is Om?
Om is your sweet home
Om is your Param Dhama,
Om is symbol of Brahman,
Om is destroyer of rebirth,   That is Om.

SACRED OM

Om is the word of power,
Om is the sacred monosyllable,

Om is the mystic letter,
Om is the Immortal Akshara.

In Om the world rests,
In Om we live and move,
In Om we go to rest,
In Om we find our quest.

Sing Om rhythmically,
Chant Om loudly,
Roar Om forcibly,
Repeat Om mentally.

Draw strength from Om,
Get inspiration from Om,
Derive energy from Om,
Imbibe bliss from Om.

Glory to Om,
Victory to Om,
Hosanna to Om,
Hail to Om.

Adorations to Om,
Salutations to Om,
Prostrations to Om,
Devotion to Om.

Rely on Om,
Reflect on Om,
Concentrate on Om,
Meditate on Om.

Om! Om!! Om!!!

NIRGUNA SONG

(Sanskrit Text is given in the preliminary pages)

1. Nirgunoham, nishkaloham,
   Nirmamoham, nischalah,
   Nitya suddho, nitya buddho
   Nirvikaro, nishkriyah.

2. Nirmaloham, kevaloham
   Ekameva advitiyah,
   Bhasuroham, bhaskaroham,
   Nityatripto chinmayah.

3. Purnakamo purnarupo,
   Purnakalo purnadik,
   Adi madhya anta hino
   Janana marana varjitah.

4. Sarvakarta sarvabhokta
   Sarvasakshi sivosmyaham,
   Sarvavyapi madvyatito
   Nasti kinchana kapyaho.

ENGLISH TRANSLATION
(Bhairavi Tune)

1. I am without qualities, without parts,
   Without mineness, immovable,
   Eternally pure, all knowing,
   Changeless and without action.

2. I am without impurity, alone
   One without a second
   Self-luminous, illuminator of everything
   With eternal satisfaction and of full knowledge.

3. I am extreme satisfaction, infinity,
   Eternity, all-pervading,

Beginningless, endless and
Free from birth and death.

4.   I am the doer in all, enjoyer in all,
The witness in all, pervader in all,
There is nothing except my own Self.

SONG OF VIRAT

Bhajo Radhe Krishna, Bhajo Radhe Shyama
Om Om Orn Om Om—Om Om Om Om Om
Soham Soham—Sivoham Soham
The whole world is my body, the shrubs are my hairs;
All bodies are mine, I enjoy in all bodies.
All mouths are mine, I eat through all these mouths;
All eyes are mine, I perceive through all these eyes.
                            (Bhajo Radhe Krishna...)

All ears are mine, I hear through all these ears;
All noses are mine, I smell through all noses,
All hands are mine, I work through all these hands;
The heaven is my head, the earth is my feet.
                            (Bhajo Radhe Krishna...)

The sun and the moon are my two eyes;
Fire is my mouth, the wind is my breath.
The space is my trunk, the ocean is my bladder,
The mountains are my bones, the rivers are my veins.
                            (Bhajo Radhe Krishna...)

Dharma is my chest, Adharma is my back,
Time is my movement, flow of Gunas is my play
Who can describe the Virat Svarupa?
It is magnanimous and soul stirring.
                            (Bhajo Radhe Krishna...)

SONG OF BLISS

Anandoham Anandoham Anandam Brahmanandam
Sacharachara Paripurna Sivoham,
Sahajananda Svarupa Sivoham
Vyapaka Chetana Atma Sivoham
Vyaktavyakta Svarupa Sivoham.

Nitya Suddha Nirmaya Soham,
Nityananda Niranjana Soham
Akhandaikarasa Chinmatroham.
Bhumananda Svarupa Sivoham.

Asangoham Advaitoham,
Vijnanaghana Chaitanyoham
Nirakara Nirguna Chinmayoham.
Suddha Satchidananda Svarupoham.

Asanga Svaprakasa Nirmaloham
Nirvisesha Chinmatra Kevaloham
Sakshi Chetana Kutasthoham
Nitya Mukta Svarupa Sivoham.

Sivaivaham Sivaivaham Sivaivaham Sivoham,
Hamsa Soham Soham Hamsa Hamsa Soham
                                    Soham Hamsa
Brahmaivaham Brahmaivaham Brahmaivaham
                                    Brahmoham
Anandoham Anandoham Anandam Brahmanandam.

SONG OF CHIDANANDA

Chidanand Chidanand Chidananda Hum,
Har Halme Almast Sat-chit-ananda Hum;

Nijanand Nijanand Nijananda Hum,
Har Halme Almast Sat-chit-ananda Hum;

Sivanand Sivanand Sivananda Hum,
Agadbhumvala Agadbhumvala Akhilananda Hum;

Ajaranand Amaranand Achalananda Hum,
Har Halme Almast Sat-chit-ananda Hum.

Antarai

Nirbhaya Aur Nischinta Chidghanananda Hum,
Kaivalya Kevala Kutastha Ananda Hum,
Nitya Suddha Siddha Sat-chit-ananda Hum.
Knowledge Bliss, Knowledge Bliss, Bliss Absolute
In all conditions, I am Knowledge Bliss Absolute.
I am without old age, without death, without motion,
In all conditions, I am Knowledge Bliss Absolute.

Antarai

I am without fear, without worry, Bliss Absolute,
Existence Absolute,
Knowledge Absolute;
Independent, unchanging, non-dual Atma,
Immortal Atma,
Advaita Atma;
Eternal, pure, perfect Knowledge Bliss Absolute
Chidanand Chidanand Chidananda Hum,
Har Halme Almast Sat-chit-ananda Hum.

SWEET OM

Om is the word of power,
Om is the sacred monosyllable,
Om is the highest Mantra,
Om is the symbol of Brahman,
Om is Soham,
Om is Om Tat Sat.
Om is the source for everything,
Om is the womb of Vedas,
Om is the basis for languages,
In Om merge all Trinities,
From Om proceed all sounds,

In Om exist all objects.
O Sweet Om! Potent Pranava!
The Life of my life,
The boat to cross this Samsara,
Harbinger of Eternal Bliss,
My Redeemer and Saviour!
Guide me and take me
To Brahman, the hidden sage!

VEDANTIC SONG

(Mettu—Are Sanyya—Hindusthani)

1. Om Antaratma,
   Nitya Suddha Buddha
   Chidakasa Kutastha.
              (Om Antaratma.)

2. Om Vyapak Svayamjyoti
   Purna Para Brahma
              (Om Antaratma.)

3. Sakshi Drashtha Turiya,
   Santam Sivam Advaitam,
   Amala Vimala Achala,
   Avang Mano Gochara.
              (Orn Antaratma.)

4. Anandame
   Chidanandame, Anandame
   Chidanandame.
   (Gopal Nandalala Bhansi Bajanevala.
              (Om Antaratma.)

SONG OF BRAHMAMAYAM

Sarvam Brahma-mayam Re Re,

                (Sarvam Brahma-mayam).

Dehonaham, Jivonaham, Pratyagabhinna

                Bramaivaham,

Paripurnoham Paramarthoham Brahmaivaham

                Brahmoham—

                (Sarvam Brahma-mayam).

Kim Vachaniyam, Kimavachaniyam,

Kim Rachaniyam, Kimarachaniyam—

                (Sarvam Brahma-mayam).

Kim Pathaniyam, Kimapathaniyam,

Kim Bhoktavyam, Kimabhoktavyam—

                (Sarvam Brahma-mayam).

Sarvatra Sada Hamsa Dhyanam,

Kartavyam Bho Mukti Nidhanam—

                (Sarvam Brahma-mayam).

Hamsa Soham Soham Hamsa,

                Hamsa Soham Soham Hamsa,

Brahmaivaham, Brahmaivaham,

                Brahmaivaham, Brahmoham,

Sivaivaham, Sivaivaham, Sivaivaham, Sivoham.

                (Sarvam Brahma-mayam).

KIRTAN
Om Dhvanis

1. Om Om Om Om Om Vichar
    Om Om Om Om Bhajo Omkar.

2. Om Tat Sat, Om Tat Sat, Om Tat Sat Om;
    Om Tat Sat, Om Tat Sat, Om Tat Sat Om.

Om Tat Sat, Om Tat Sat, Om Tat Sat Om;
Om Santi, Om Santi, Om Santi Om.

Antarai

Om Tat Sat, Om Tat Sat, Om Tat Sat Om;
Hari Om Tat Sat, Sri Om Tat Sat,
        Siva Om Tat Sat Om. (Om Tat Sat.)

3. Om Om Om Om Om, Om Om Om Om Om,
        Om Om Om Om Om, Om Om Om
Om Soham Sivoham, Soham Sivoham,
        Soham Sivoham, Sivoham.
Soham Sivoham, Aham Brahmasmi,
        Sat-chit-ananda Svarupa Sivoham.
Atma Brahma Svarupa, Chaitanya Purusha,
        Tejomayananda Tat-tvam-asi Lakshya.
Prajnanam Brahma, Aham Brahmasmi,
        Tat-tvam-asi, Ayamatma Brahma.
Satyam Sivam Subham Sundaram Kantam,
        Sat-chit-ananda Sampurna (Sukha) Santam.
Om Om Om Om Om, Om Om Om Om Om,
        Om Om Om Om Om, Om Om Om.

CHAPTER VI

GARLAND OF OM

CHHANDOGYA UPANISHAD

Om, the Udgitha, to be meditated upon; because people sing with Om in the beginning. Its explanation (is as follows):

The earth constitutes the essence of all these beings; water is the essence of the earth; herbs of water; man forms the essence of herbs; speech of man; Rik is the essence of speech; Sama of Rik; and the Udgitha of Sama.

The Essence of essences is the Udgitha; it is the supreme, the most adorable, the eighth.

What is Rik? What is Sama? What is Udgitha? These are explained (now):

Rik is speech; Sama is the vital breath; the syllable Om is the Udgitha. Verily, speech and breath or Rik and Sama form a couple.

As couple when united are mutually gratified of their desires, so this couple unites with the letter Om.

Verily he alone fulfills the desires, who knowing thus, meditates upon this syllable as the Udgitha.

This is verily a syllable of acquiescence. Whenever we acquiesce in anything, Om is repeated; hence this is gratification. Knowing thus, he who adores the Udgitha becomes the gratifier of desires.

Through its greatness does the threefold science proceed; one recites with Om, orders with Om and chants with Om—all this for the worship of Om.

He who knows and he who does not know alike perform actions through this syllable. Knowledge and ignorance are different. That which is performed through knowledge, faith and meditation is more effective. Verily this is the explanation of the syllable. (Chapter I-i-1 to 10)

This letter Om ought to be meditated upon, because one recites beginning with Om. Its description (is as follows):

Fearing death, the Devas adopted the threefold knowledge of the Vedas. They protected themselves with the metrical hymns. Because they shielded themselves thus, these hymns are called *chhandas*.

Just as one would see a fish in water, so did death behold the Devas in the Rik, Yajus and Saman hymns. Knowing this, the Devas arose from the Vedas and entered the asylum of voice—*svara* (Om).

When one recites the Rik, he loudly chants Om; the same with the Yajus and Sama; and therefore this accent (Svara), the syllable Om is immortal and fearless. Taking its support, the Devas became immortal and secure.

He who knowing thus praises this letter, enters the syllable, the *svada*, the immortal and fearless, and obtaining it becomes immortal like the Devas. (Chapter I-iv-1 to 4)

Verily that which is Udgitha is Pranava (Om) and that which is Pranava is Udgitha. The Aditya (sun) is the Udgitha and also Pranava because he moves along resounding Om.

"Verily I sang in praise of the sun," said Kaushitaki to his son: "therefore thou art my only one; do thou reflect upon the rays and thou shalt obtain many sons." This is with reference to Devas.

Next with reference to the body; verily one ought to meditate upon the Udgitha, the breath of the mouth, for it proceeds resounding Om.

"Verily, I sang in praise of breath; do thou sing in praise of it as manifold, praying for numerous sons"—said thus Kaushitaki to his son.

Verily he who knows the Udgitha to be the Pranava and the Pranava to be the Udgitha rectifies by the rituals of the Hotri, the errors of Udgitha—verily, rectifies the errors of the Udgitha: (Chapter I-v-1 to 5)

The division of duty is threefold: Sacrifice, reading of the Vedas and charity constitute the first; austerity is the second and the third is life of student exclusively in the house of the Guru. All those (who act in these ways) attain the virtuous regions—but only the firm believer in Brahman attains Immortality.

Prajapati reflected on these words; from them this knowledge issued forth. He reflected on it and from the reflected, Bhuh, Bhuvah and Svah issued forth.

He brooded upon them and from them issued forth Om. As all leaves are attached to the stalks, so is the speech connected to the syllable Om. Om verily is all this; verily all this is Om. (Chapter II-xxiii—1 to 3)

KATHOPANISHAD

Yama said: "The goal (word) which all the Vedas speak of (praise) which all penances proclaim and wishing for which they lead the life of a Brahmacharin, that goal (word) I will briefly tell thee—It is Om.

This word is verily Brahman; this word is verily the highest; he who knows this word, obtains, verily whatever he desires.

This is the best support. This is the highest support. He who knows this support is worshipped in the world of Brahman." (Chapter II-15 to 17)

PRASNOPANISHAD

Then Satyakama, son of Sibi, questioned him (Pippalada): "O Bhagavan! If some one among men meditates here until death on the syllable Om, what world does he attain by that?"

He replied: "O Satyakama! The syllable Om is indeed the higher and the lower Brahman. Therefore he who knows it, by this means, surely attains either of them.

"If he meditates on the Matra (measure) 'A,' then he being enlightened by that comes quickly to earth. The Rik verses lead him to the world of men, and being endowed there with austerity, celibacy and faith, he enjoys greatness.

"But if he meditates on its second Matra only, he becomes one with the mind. He is led up by the Yajus-verses to the sky, the world of the moon. Having enjoyed greatness there, he returns again.

"But if again he meditates on the Highest Purusha, with this syllable Om of three Matras, he becomes united with the highest sun. As a snake is freed from its slough, so is he freed from sin. He is led up by the Sama-verses to the world of Brahma (Hiranyagarbha), and from him, full of life he learns to see the all-pervading, the highest Person. There are the two following verses:

"The three Matras which employed separately are mortal; but (when they are) connected with one another, they are not wrongly employed. When they are properly employed, in all the internal, external and middle functions, the knower trembles not.

"Through the Rik-verses he arrives at this world, through the Yajus-verses at the sky, through the Sama-verses at that which the seers know (the Brahmaloka); he arrives at this by means of the letter Om: the wise arrive at that which is quiet, undecaying, deathless, fearless and supreme." (V-1 to 7)

BRIHADARANYAKA UPANISHAD

Om is ether, Om is Brahman. The ether exists of old, the ether is the source of the wind; thus said the son of Kauravyayani. This Om is the Veda, thus the Brahmanas know. One knows through it all that has to be known. (Chapter V-i-1)

MUNDAKA UPANISHAD

Having taken the bow supplied by the Upanishads, the great weapon, and fixed in it the arrow sharpened by incessant meditation and having drawn it with the mind fixed on Brahman, hit O gentle youth! at that mark, the immortal Brahman.

Pranava Om is the bow, the Atman is the arrow, and the Brahman is called its aim. It is to be hit by a man who is self-collected (with concentration) and then as the arrow becomes one with the target he will become one with Brahman.

He moves about becoming manifold within the heart where the nerves meet, like spokes fastened to the nave of the wheel; meditate on Om as the Self. Hail to you, that you may go to the other side beyond darkness. (II-ii-3, 4 and 6)

TAITTIRIYA UPANISHAD

May He, the Lord of all, pre-eminent among the Vedas (in the form of Om), more immortal than the immortal Vedas, bless me with wisdom. May I be adorned with the knowledge of Brahman that leads to immortality. May my body become strong and vigorous (for practising meditation on Brahman with the *japa* of Om). May my tongue always utter sweet words. May I hear much with my ears. Thou (Om) art the sheath of Brahma hidden by intelligence. May Thou protect what I have heard.

O Venerable! Let me enter Thee (Om) the sheath of Brahman, *svaha*. May Thou, O Venerable, enter me, *svaha*. I shall be cleansed, O Venerable, by Thee of thousand branches, *svaha*. (I-iv-1 and 3)

SVETASVATARA UPANISHAD

As the nature of fire when concealed in its cause, the wood, is not perceived, and is again and again perceived without undergoing destruction of its subtle body (in the art of rubbing), so is the soul pervaded manifestly within the body by the sacred word Om.

Making his own body the lower piece of wood and the sacred Pranava Om the upper piece, one should, practising meditation as the rubbing, realise God, as the concealed fire through percussion is made visible. (Chapter 1-13 and 14)

Holding the upper part of the body erect, and also the other part steady, subduing the senses and the mind within the heart, one should with the raft of Brahman Om cross over all the fearful (worldly) currents.

SANDILYA UPANISHAD

"One should meditate on that single letter, the supreme light. The Pranava is the origin or source of these three letters, 'A', 'U, 'M."

DHYANABINDU UPANISHAD

The one Akshara (letter Om) should be contemplated upon as Brahman by all who aspire for emancipation. Prithvi, Agni, Rigveda, Bhuh and Brahma—all these (are absorbed) when Akara (A), the first part of Pranava Om becomes absorbed. Antariksha, Yajurveda, Vayu, Bhuvah and Vishnu (Janardana)—all these (are absorbed) when Ukara (U), the second part of Pranava becomes absorbed. Dyuh, Sun, Samaveda, Suvah and Mahesvara—all these (are absorbed) when Makara (M) the third part of Pranava becomes absorbed. Akara is of yellow colour and is said to be of Rajoguna; Ukara is of white colour and of Sattvaguna;

Makara is of dark colour and of Tamoguna. He who does not know Omkara, as having eight parts, four feet, three seats and five presiding deities, is not a Brahmana. Pranava is the bow, the Atman is the arrow, and Brahman is said to be the aim. One should aim at It with great care and then he, like the arrow, becomes one with It. When that Highest is cognised, all Karmas return (from him, viz., do not affect him). The Vedas have Omkara as their cause. The Svaras (sounds) have Omkara as their cause. The three words with (all) the locomotive and the fixed (ones in them) have Omkara as their cause. The short (accent of Om) burns all sins, the long one is decayless and the bestower of prosperity. United with Ardhamatra, the Pranava becomes the bestower of salvation. That man is the knower of the Vedas who knows that the end, viz., Ardhamatra of Pranava should be worshipped (or recited) as uninterrupted as the flow of oil and (resounding) as long as the sound of a bell. One should contemplate upon Omkara as Isvara resembling as unshaken light, as of the pericarp of the lotus of the heart. Taking in air through the left nostril and filling the stomach with it, one should contemplate upon Omkara as being in the middle of the body and as surrounded by circling flames. Brahma is said to be inspiration; Vishnu is said to he cessation (of breath) and Rudra is said to be expiration. These are the Devatas of Pranayama. Having made the Atman as the (lower) Arani (sacrificial wood) and Pranava as the upper Arani, one should see the God in secret through the practice of churning which is Dhyana. One should practise restraint of breath as much as it lies in his power along with (the uttering of) Omkara sound, until it ceases completely. Those who look upon Om as of the form of Hamsa staying in all, shining like crores of suns, being alone, staying in Gama-agama (ever going and coming) and being devoid of motion at last, such persons are freed from sin. That Manas which is the author of the actions, viz., creation, preservation and destruction of the three worlds, is (then) absorbed (in the Supreme One). That is the highest state of Vishnu.

NARADAPARIVRAJAKA UPANISHAD

Then Narada asked Parameshti (Brahma) to enlighten him who had surrendered himself to Him, about Samsara-taraka (that Taraka or Pranava which lifts one out of Samsara).

Assenting to it Brahma began thus: "Omkara that is Brahman is the Vyashti (individual) and the Samashti (cosmic). What is the individual? What is the cosmic? Brahma Pranava is of three kinds, Samhara destructive, Srishti creative and Ubhayatmaka belonging to both. It is also eight: Antah-pranava, Vyavaharika-pranava, Bahya-pranava, Arsha-pranava, Ubhayatmaka or Virat-pranava, Samhara-pranava, Brahmapranava and Ardhamatra-pranava. Om is Brahman. Know that the one-syllabled Mantra of Akara, Ukara, Makara and Ardhamatra, Nada, Bindu, Kala and Sakti. Akara is associated with ten thousand limbs; Ukara is with one thousand limbs; Makara with one hundred limbs; Ardhamatra is of the nature of endless limbs. That which is Saguna (associated with Gunas) is Virat (preservation) Pranava; that which Nirguna (not associated with Gunas) is Samhara (destruction) Pranava; that which is associated with Gunas and is not so associated, is Utpatti (origination) Pranava. Pluta (the elongated accent) is Virat; Pluta-pluta is Samhara. The Virat-pranava is of the form of sixteen Matras and is above the thirty-six Tattvas. The sixteen Matras are thus: Akara is the first Matra; Ukara is the second; Makara is the third; Ardhamatra is the fourth; Nada is the fifth; Bindu is the sixth; Kala is the seventh; Kalatita is the eighth; Santi is the ninth; Santyatita is the tenth; Unmani is the eleventh; Manonmani is the twelfth; Puritati is the thirteenth; Tanumadhyama is the fourteenth; Pasyanti is the fifteenth; Para is the sixteenth. Then (again) having sixty-four Matras and their division into the two, Prakriti and Purusha and resolving themselves into the one hundred and twenty-eight differences of Matras, it becomes Saguna and Nirguna. Though Brahma Pranava is one only, it is the substratum for all, the support of the whole universe, of the form of all Aksharas (letters), time, Vedas and Siva. This Omkara that is mentioned in the Vedas of the nature of the Upanishads, should be sought after. Know that this Omkara is the Atman that is indestructible during the three periods of time, past, present and future, able to confer salvation and eulogised by Vedas. Having experienced this one Om, immortal, ageless, and having brought about the Brahman-nature in this body, become convinced that your Atman associated with the three bodies, is Parabrahman.

MANU SMRITI

The syllable Om should be pronounced before the beginning and ending the study of Vedas; for unless it is pronounced at the beginning and the end the learning will be easily forgotten.

From the three Vedas (Rik, Yajus and Sama) Brahma milked out the letters 'A,' 'U' and 'M,' together with the mysterious symbols, Bhuh, Bhuvah and Svah.

A knower of the Vedas who pronounces this syllable (OM) both morning and evening along with that holy text (Gayatri) proceeded by the three words (Vyahriti) shall attain the place which the Vedas confer.

A twice-born man who repeats all the three (Om, Vyahriti and Gayatri) in a quiet place shall be released in a month from any great offence like a snake from its slough.

The Om syllable is the *svarupa* (emblem) of Parabrahman (Supreme).

Oblations to fire, sacrifices, etc., ordained by the Vedas shall pass away; but the OM syllable which is the symbol of the supreme does not pass away and hence it is called Akshara.

PATANJALI YOGA SUTRAS

The sacred syllable Om connotes Him (Isvara).

Its repetition and its meditation with meaning should be practised.

Then comes the cognition of the individual soul and also the removal of all obstacles. (1-27 to 29)

SRIMAD BHAGAVAD GITA

I am the syllable Om in all the Vedas. (VII-8)

That which is declared Imperishable by Veda-knowers, that which the self-controlled and passion-free enter, that desiring which Brahmacharya is practised—that goal I will declare to thee in brief.

Having closed all the gates, having confined the mind in the heart, having fixed the life-breath in the head, engaged in the practice of concentration, uttering the one-syllable Om—the Brahman, and remembering Me, he who departs, leaving the body, attains the Supreme Goal. (VIII-11 to 13)

CHAPTER VII

MANDUKYOPANISHAD

ॐ भद्रं कर्णेभिः श्रृणुयाम देवाः भद्रं पश्येमाक्षभिर्यजत्राः ।
स्थिरैरङ्गैस्तुष्टुवा ँसस्तनूभिर्व्यशेम देवहितं यदायुः ।। स्वस्ति न इन्द्रो वृद्धश्रवाः
स्वस्ति नः पूषाः विश्ववेदाः । स्वस्ति नस्ताक्ष्यों अरिष्टनेमिः स्वस्ति नो
बृहस्पतिर्दधातु ।।

ॐ शान्तिः शान्तिः शान्तिः ।।

Om bhadram karnebhih srinuyama devah
bhadram pasyemakshabhiryajatrah,
Sthirairangaistushtuvamsa-stanubhih
vyasema devahitam yadayuh.

Svasti na indro vriddhasravah
svasti nah pushah visvavedah,
Svasti nastarkshyo arishtanemih
svasti no brihaspatirdadhatu.

Om Santih, Santih, Santih.

Om, O gods, may we, with our ears, hear what is auspicious; O ye! fit to be worshipped, may we, with our eyes, see
what is auspicious; may we enjoy the life allotted to us by the
gods, offering our praise with our bodies strong of limb. May
Indra, the powerful, the ancient of fame, vouchsafe us prosperity. May He, the nourisher and the possessor of all wealth,

92

give us what is well for us. May the Lord of swift motion be propitious to us, and may the protector of the great ones protect us too.

Om Peace, Peace, Peace.

हरि: ॐ ! ओमित्येतदक्षरमिद ँ सर्वं तस्योपव्याख्यानं भूतं भवद्भविष्यदिति सर्वमोङ्कार एव। यच्चान्यत्त्रिकालातीतं तदप्योङ्कार एव ॥१॥

ॐ — Om, इति — thus, एतत् — this, अक्षरं — word, इदं — this, सर्वं — all, तस्य — its, उपव्याख्यानं — explanation, भूतं — the past, भवत् — the present, भविष्यत् — the future, इति — thus, सर्वं — all, ओंकार — the Om, एव — verily, यत् — what, च — and, अन्यत् — the other, त्रिकालातीतं — beyond the threefold time, तत् — that, अपि — also, ओंकार — Om, एव — verily.

1. Om, the word, is all this. Its further explanation is this. All that is past, present and future is verily Om. That which is beyond the triple conception of time, is verily Om.

In this Upanishad, Varuna, the Lord of Waters assumes the form of a frog (*Manduka*) and praises Om. Varuna is the Rishi or Revealer of this Upanishad. Brahman is the Devata; Anushtup is the metre. The person qualified to study this Upanishad is anyone who wants to attain liberation.

Om, the Pranava, the Omkara is the only symbol of Brahman, the Absolute. Just as a sick man regains his equilibrium when the cause of the disease vanishes, so also the Jiva, the individual soul regains his equilibrium, the original state of pristine glory or divine splendour, oneness or unity with the Supreme Self when the illusion of duality caused by ignorance is destroyed by the knowledge of the Self.

The sacred monosyllable Om is the only name of Brahman, the Supreme Soul. Brahman is nameless but in the relative plane a name is necessary for giving instructions to the aspirants. Even the highest Brahman is realised by means of a name only.

Name is a symbol or representative of the person or thing named. Name of a person or a thing denotes the person or thing of which it is the name. The words 'Buddha,' 'Rama' are the names of certain persons who lived at certain periods of time. These words are the symbols of those persons. A picture of a person or a thing is also a symbol of the person or the thing which it represents. When you look at the photo or picture of a person, you give a description of the person by naming the person. The name of a person is remembered for a very long time. We still remember the names of Lord Jesus, Lord Rama, Sri Sankara and others. The person dies but the name lives for ever. Therefore the name is more comprehensive than the picture.

"Om is this;" "Om is the support;" "Om is Brahman;" "Om is the Akshara, the Immortal;" "Om is the Atman;" "Om is pure Chaitanya Consciousness;" "The word Om is all;" "One should, with purity of heart, fix his mind on the Atman through Om which is the Atman"—these texts of the Upanishads declare that Om, Brahman and the Atman are one and the same.

The famous Mantra of Sri Guru Nanak begins with "*Sat Nam Ek Omkar*," i.e., Real Name, One Om. Om is this all. It clearly means that Brahman or the Supreme Self denoted by the syllable Om is this all. Its explanation should be known. What was, what is, and what will be, all is verily the word Om. Every object has a name. The name and the object denoted by it are identical. All objects are not different from their names. The connection between *sabda* (sound) and *artha* (object) is inseparable. Names and forms are inseparable.

Name is a sound-symbol. Thoughts cannot he separated from forms and names. Brahman willed. There was Brahma-sankalpa: "May I become many." There was a Spandan, vibration. Then creation began. This original vibration or sound-symbol is Om. This Om is the most universal, all-inclusive sound. All names are not different from Om, because Om is the basis or matrix for all sounds, words and names. Therefore, it is proper to say that all this is indeed Om. Om is the right symbol of Brahman. Through Om alone you will have to approach Brahman. Just as heat is inseparable from fire, just as fragrance is inseparable from the flower, so also Om is inseparable from Brahman. Om is a means to the knowledge of Brahman. Om is the means by which the Immortal Self, denoted by Om is realised. Om is very intimately related to Brahman. Om is very near to Brahman. Om is in the vicinity of Brahman. If you know Om, you know Brahman also. Therefore it is very necessary to have a comprehensive understanding of Om. A clear explanation of Om is very essential. A very lucid and elaborate explanation is given in this Upanishad. The Karikas of Sri Gaudapadacharya are very illuminating. The method of approach to Brahman through the sacred monosyllable Om is very clearly enunciated in this remarkable Upanishad which is an abridgment or a short summary of all the hundred and eight Upanishads.

Just as an object is known through its names, so also Brahman, the Supreme Self, is known through Om alone. If anyone utters the words, 'that is a mango tree,' you at once know all about the mango tree, its leaves, flowers, fruits, nature of the fruits, benefits of the fruits, etc., through the name 'mango tree.' Just as you know all about mango through the name 'mango,' so also you can know all about Brahman through Om alone. Therefore, Brahman is indeed Om. Brahman, the Atman, Chaitanya, Purushottama, Svarupa, Supreme Self and Om are identical.

The sacred monosyllable Om denotes the all-pervading immortal, indivisible, self-luminous, unchanging Brahman, the Supreme Self of which it is a name.

Akshara: This word means that which is imperishable or immortal, that which does not decay or decompose. It also means a letter of the alphabet. In the Gita you will find, "*Aksharanam Akarosmi* amongst all the letters, I am the letter 'A' " (X-33). It also means the monosyllable *Ekaksharam* Om (X-25). The word 'Akshara' here clearly means the monosyllable Om, but not the immortal Brahman.

Tasya: of Om.

Upavyakhyanam: clear explanation.

All that is subject to the threefold time such as past, present and future (manifold) is verily Om or Brahman. All that is beyond the triple conceptions of time (unmanifest—Avyakrita)) and yet present in Consciousness through its effects, is also verily Om, is not apart from Om. Brahman is denoted by the word Om. Brahman is above the three periods of time (Trikalatita). Therefore, Om also is beyond the three periods of time. That which is beyond three periods of time, is Om alone. Om means literally that by which everything is pervaded (Otam). This word Om is woven in Brahman like warp and woof and, therefore, denotes Brahman. That which enters into everything is Om.

Just as the rope is the substratum for the illusion of snake, so also Om is the substratum for the illusion of speech. All is mere play of words. Ideas or thoughts are communicated through words only. Experiences are expressed through words only. Incidents are narrated through words only. Everything is held together by 'the string of speech, by the cord, rope or thread of specific names. The world cannot exist without names or words. The world cannot run without names or words. Therefore, it is proper to say that 'All is the word.'

Names cannot exist apart from Om which is Brahman. Brahman is one with Om. The Atman is one with Om.

This treatise is the explanation of this Om, the word (Akshara) which is of the same nature as the higher Brahman without attributes as well as the lower Brahman with attributes.

सर्व ँ ह्येतद्ब्रह्मायमात्मा ब्रह्म सोऽयमात्मा चतुष्पात् ॥२॥

सर्व — all, हि — verily, एतत् — this ब्रह्म — Brahman अयं — this, आत्मा — the Atman (the Supreme Self), ब्रह्म — Brahman, सः — that (he), अयं — this, आत्मा — the Atman, चतुष्पात् — is with four quarters (four feet, portions, aspects or conditions).

2. All this is verily Brahman. This Atman (the Supreme Self) is Brahman. This Atman has four quarters (four feet, portions, aspects or conditions).

This Atman called Om is Para (higher) Brahman as well as Apara (lower) Brahman and has four quarters, four feet, not like those of a cow, but like the fractions of a coin.

The Sanskrit word Pada literally means foot. In this first Mantra, it is said that Om the word is all this. In this Mantra it is said 'All this is verily Brahman.' This clearly denotes that Om is Brahman.

All this is verily Brahman: all—the manifested and the unmanifested world comprised in the word 'all'—is Brahman. All that has been declared to consist of Om in the above Mantra is Brahman. In the previous text the whole of the objective manifestation has been said to be of the form of Om or Brahman.

In this Mantra it is said that Brahman is not only the visible, manifested world but also the very innermost Self or the Atman.

This Atman is Brahman. Brahman cannot he demonstrated. But it is possible to infer its existence from certain empirical facts. The existence of Brahman is inferred or known on the ground of its being the self of everyone. For, everyone is conscious of the existence of his self and never thinks 'I am not.' If the existence of the Self were not known, everyone would think 'I am not.' And this Self of whose existence all are conscious, is Brahman. That Brahman whose existence is inferred by certain empirical facts, by the study of the Upanishads, is now pointed out as being directly cognised or realised by the text, "*Ayam Atma Brahma*—this self or *jivatma* is Brahman." The word Atma means that which pervades all.

Direct realisation of Brahman (Aparoksha Anuhhuti) is pointed out here. The author or the seer points out with his forefinger to the region of the heart or breast. 'this Atman is Brahman.' People have generally got the belief that the region of the heart is the seat or abode of the Atman, Brahman, the Soul. That is the reason why the seer points out with his forefinger to the region of the heart. The words 'this Atman' indicates something very near. A sage is a seer who possesses direct intuitional knowledge of Brahman. He knows Brahman through Self-realisation (Atma-sakshatkara). Just as one knows the Amalaka fruit in his hand, so also he knows Brahman. That is the reason why he declares with certainty with a gesture of hand, "this Atman is Brahman."

There are four Mahavakyas or great sentences in the Upanishads. Each Veda contains one Mahavakya. "*Ayam Atma Brahma*—This Atman is Brahman" is the fourth Mahavakya. This is contained in this Mandukya Upanishad of the Atharva Veda. This is Anubhavabodha-vakya, the great text or the great sentence that gives expression to the inner intuitive experience or Aparoksha Anubhuti, the direct per-

ception of the innermost self by the aspirant through meditation (Nididhyasana). This Mahavakya denotes the identity or
oneness of the individual soul, with Brahman, the Supreme
Soul. The other three Mahavakyas are:

1. "*Prajnanam Brahma*—Consciousness is Brahman."
This is Svarupa-bodha-vakya, the great sentence that ex-
plains the nature of Brahman, the Self. This is contained in
the Aitareya Upanishad of the Rig-veda.

2. "*Aham Brahmasmi*—I am Brahman." This is
Anusandhana-vakya. The aspirant tries to fix his mind on the
idea 'I am Brahman.' This is contained in the Brihadaranyaka
Upanishad of the Yajur-veda.

3. "*Tat-tvam-asi*—Thou   art   That."   This   is
Upadesa-vakya. The teacher instructs the student "my child,
Thou art That, Thou art Brahman. Realise this and be free."
This is contained in the Chhandogya Upanishad of the
Sama-veda.

Chatushpad: four feet; four quarters; Pada means foot
or instrument. Visva (Jagrat Avastha, the waking state),
Taijasa (Svapna Avastha, the dreaming state), Prajna
(Sushupti Avastha, the state of deep sleep) and Turiya,
superconsciousness which is same as Brahman, the Atman,
Atman are the four feet or the four conditions

Just as a quarter-coin is merged in the half-coin, the half
is resolved in the three-fourth and the three quarters is finally
resolved in the full coin so also Visva is resolved in Taijasa,
Taijasa in Prajna, and ultimately Prajna is merged in Turiya.
The fourth is realised by merging the other three states in it, in
the order of the lower in the higher. The word quarter means
here an 'instrument' that helps one for the realisation of the
fourth, the Turiya.

Visva is the individual soul who experiences the gross
objects in the waking state. Visva is the reflected intelligence
(Chaitanya, Chidabhasa). Taijasa is the reflected Chaitanya,
the individual soul who experiences the dream objects in the

dreaming state. Prajna is the individual soul, the reflected Chaitanya or intelligence who experiences the bliss of deep sleep state. Visva, Taijasa and Prajna are one. The experience of Prajna in deep sleep is expressed by Visva in the waking state. It is Visva who says: "I enjoyed sound sleep last night. I did not know anything."

जागरितस्थानो बहिष्प्रज्ञः सप्ताङ्ग एकोनविंशतिमुखः स्थूलभुग्वैश्वानरः प्रथमः पादः ॥३॥

जागरितस्थानः — Whose sphere is the state of waking, बहिः प्रज्ञः — whose consciousness is outward, सप्ताङ्गः — seven-limbed, एकोनविंशतिमुखः — nineteen-mouthed, स्थूलभुक् — ennoyer of gross objects, वैश्वानरः — Vaisvanara, प्रथमः— first, पादः — foot or quarter or condition.

3. The first quarter is Vaisvanara whose sphere is the state of waking, who is conscious of the external objects, who has seven limbs and nineteen mouths and who enjoys the gross objects.

The text now begins to explain how Om is made up of four quarters. Through the force of Avidya or ignorance, the Visva, the individual soul in the waking state enjoys the gross objects of the external visible world.

The seven limbs are members:

1. Heaven is the head of Vaisvanara or Visva.

2. The sun and the moon are His eyes.

3. Air is His breath.

4. Fire (Ahavaniya fire, one of the three fires of the Agnihotra sacrifice) is His mouth.

5. Sky is His middle or body.

6. Water is His urinary organ (kidney or bladder).

7. Earth is His feet.

The nineteen mouths are:

1. The five Jnana Indriyas, organs of knowledge (sensory organs) are ear, skin, eye, tongue and nose. Sound, touch, form, taste and smell are experienced by these five organs respectively.

2. The five Karma Indriyas, organs of actions (motor organs) are mouth (organ of speech), hands, feet, generative organ and anus, the excretory organ.

3. The five Pranas or vital airs are *prana, apana, samana, vyana* and *udana.*

4. The fourfold Antahkarana consists of Manas (mind), Buddhi (intellect), Chitta (subconscious mind or the faculty by which things are remembered) and Ahamkara (egoism or self-arrogating principle).

These nineteen are called mouths because through these the Jivatma enjoys the external gross things of the objective universe. These are the avenues of knowledge and experience. The text gives here a description of Vaisvanara or Visva and not the Virat. Virat is the universal or the macrocosmic aspect of Isvara and Visva is the individual or microcosmic aspect. The sum total of all Visva is Virat. Jiva is a microcosm of the great macrocosm. The meaning of the common saying, "*Joi pinde soi brahmande*" is "whatever exists in one's own body also exists in the universe." Physical body of the Jiva is also the body of the Virat. The whole world is the body of the Virat-purusha. The sum total of the physical bodies is Virat. The totality of the gross universe is Virat. The human body is a miniature universe. The astral body (Linga Deha, Sukshma Deha) of the Jiva or the individual soul is also the astral body of Hiranyagarbha. The causal body (Karana Sarira) of the Jiva is also the Karana Sarira of Isvara. Jiva is not separate from Virat, Hiranyagarbha and Isvara. The sum total of all subtle bodies is Hiranyagarbha. The sum total of all causal bodies is Isvara.

The members and organs of the individual souls are also the members and organs of the universal soul.

Vaisvanara: Nara means leads; it leads all Visva in the same direction, viz., enjoyment of the gross external objects; or it means all beings, Nara means a collective name for all beings on the objective plane. Jagrat is that state during which the individual soul enjoys the gross objects of senses through the nineteen organs, having the sun and the rest as their presiding deities. The Jagrat Avastha, the wakeful state is the last state in the evolution of the universe, but it is the first state in the order of involution. The dreaming state and the state of deep sleep follow the wakeful state, which quarter is called first with reference to experience but not with reference to the order of evolution or creation. This is called the first because all the other quarters or conditions are approached or realised through this, and because from the waking state only the dream state and the deep sleep state are known.

From a study of the waking state, you will have to proceed to the study of dream and deep sleep states. When you begin to analyse this universe for the sake of realising the Atman, you will have to deal with the wakeful state first. Therefore, this is called the first quarter or the first condition. To begin with, you will have to understand the nature of the gross objects. Then you can gradually go to the subtle and causal nature of things. You will have to render the mind sharp and subtle through meditation and discipline it in order to comprehend the subtle and causal nature of things.

Vaisvanara is one with Virat on the physical plane. Taijasa is one with Hiranyagarbha on the astral or subtle plane. Prajna is one with Isvara on the causal plane. When the illusion of duality vanishes you will very easily realise the unity of the Atman and Brahman. *Sarvam Khalvidam Brahma*—all indeed is Brahman. There is no such thing as diversity. You will fully realise the truth of the Upanishadic texts, 'The Atman is one in all,' 'All is in the one' and 'He who beholds all in the Self.' This unity or oneness is described in the Madhu-brahmana of the Brihadaranyaka Upanishad also. The Tejomaya (resplendent or self-effulgent) Purusha in this earth and the Amritamaya (immortal) Purusha in this body are both the same.

Virat, under the orders of Isvara, having entered this microcosmic body and having the intellect as his vehicle, reaches the state of Visva. Then he goes by the several names of Vijnanatma, Chidabhasa, Visva, Vyavaharic Jiva, the one presiding over the waking gross body and the one generated by Karma.

स्वप्नस्थानोऽन्तःप्रज्ञः सप्ताङ्ग एकोनविंशतिमुखः प्रविविक्तभुक्तैजसो द्वितीयः पादः ॥४॥

स्वप्नस्थानः — Whose sphere or field or place is dream, अन्तःप्रज्ञः — whose consciousness is inward, सप्ताङ्गः — seven limbed, एकोनविंशतिमुखः — nineteen-mouthed, प्रविविक्तभुक् — enjoyer of the subtle objects, तैजसः — the taijasa, द्वितीयः— the second, पादः— quarter.

4. The second quarter is the Taijasa whose sphere or field or place is dream, who is conscious of internal objects, who has seven limbs and nineteen mouths and enjoys the subtle objects.

During dream, the mind creates various kinds of objects out of the impressions produced by the experiences of the waking state. The mind reproduces the whole of its waking life in dream through the force of Avidya (ignorance), Kama (desire and imagination) and Karma (action). The mind is the perceiver and the mind itself is the perceived in the dream. The mind creates the objects without the help of any external means. It creates various curious, fantastic mixtures. You may witness in the dream that your living father is dead, that you are flying in the air. You may see in the dream a lion with the head of an elephant, a cow with the head of a dog. The desires that are not satisfied during the waking state are gratified in dream. Dream is a mysterious phenomenon. It is more interesting than the waking state.

Dream is that state during which the Atman (Taijasa) experiences through the mind associated with the Vasanas of the waking condition, sound and other objects which are of the form of the Vasanas created for the time being, even in the absence of the gross sound and the others. Like a business man tired of worldly acts, in the waking state the individual soul strives to find the path to retire into his abode within. The Svapna Avastha is that in which, when the senses are at rest, there is the manifestation of the knower and the known along with the affinities (Vasanas) of things enjoyed in the waking state. In this state Visva alone, his actions in the waking state having ceased, reaches the state of Taijasa (of Tejas, effulgence or essence of light), who moves in the middle of the Nadis (nerves), illuminates by his lustre, the heterogenity of the subtle dream world which is of the form of Vasanas (affinities) and himself enjoys according to his wish.

Sutratma or Hiranyagarbha, under the orders of Isvara, having entered the microcosmic subtle body and having the mind as his vehicle, reaches the Taijasa state. Then he goes by the names of Taijasa, Pratibhasika and Svapnakalpita.

The dreamer creates a world of his own in the dreaming state. Mind alone works independently in this state. The senses are withdrawn into the mind. The senses are at rest. Just as a man withdraws himself from the outside world, closes the door and windows of his room and works within the room, so also the mind withdraws itself from the outside world and plays in the dream world, with the Vasanas and the Samskaras and enjoys objects made up of fine or subtle ideas which are the products of desire. Dream is a mere play of the mind only. The mind itself projects all sorts of subtle objects from its own body through the potentiality of impressions of the waking state and enjoys these objects. Therefore, there is a very subtle experience by Taijasa in the form of Vasanas only, whereas the experience of the waking state by Visva is gross.

You will find in the Brihadaranyaka Upanishad IV-iii-9: "He sleeps with full of the impressions produced by the varied experience of the waking state and experiences dreams. He takes with him the impressions of the world during the waking state, destroys and builds them up again and experiences dream by his own light." The Atharvana-veda says: "All these are in the mind. They are experienced or cognised by the Taijasa." The experiencer of the dream state is called Taijasa, because he is entirely of the essence of light.

Just as pictures are painted on the canvas, so also the impressions of the waking state are painted in the canvas-mind. The pictures on the canvas seem to possess various dimensions though it is on a plane surface only. Even so, though the dream-experiences are really states of the mind only, the experiencer experiences internality and externality in the dream world. He feels while dreaming that the dream world is quite real.

Pravivikta: Pra—differentiated; Vivikta—from the objects of the waking state. The objects perceived in the waking state have an external reality common to all beings, whereas the objects perceived in dreams are revivals of impressions received in the waking state and have an external reality only to the dreamer.

Antahprajna: inward consciousness; the experiencer is conscious of the dream-world only; subtle is that which manifests itself in dreams, being impressions of objects perceived in the waking state. The state of consciousness by which these subtle objects are perceived is called Antahprajna or inner perception. The impressions of the waking state remain in the mind which independent of the senses, are perceived in the dream. The mind is more internal than the senses. The dreamer is conscious of the mental states which are the impressions left in the mind by the previous waking state. Hence it is called Antahprajna.

The microcosmic aspect of Atman in the subtle or mental state is called Taijasa and His microcosmic aspect is known as Hiranyagarbha. Just as Virat is one with Visva in the waking state, so also Taijasa is one with Hiranyagarbha in the dreaming state.

यत्र सुप्तो न कंचन कामं कामयते न कंचन स्वप्नं पश्यति तत्सुषुप्तम् । सुषुप्तस्थान एकीभूतः प्रज्ञानघन एवानन्दमयो ह्यानन्दभुक्चेतोमुखः प्राज्ञस्तृतीयः पादः ।।५ ।।

यत्र — Where सुप्तः — sleeping (man), न — not, कंचन — any कामं — desire (or object of desire), कामयते — desires for, न — not कंचन — any स्वप्नं — dream, पश्यति — sees, तत् — that, सुषुप्तम्— the deep sleep, सुषुप्तस्थानः — whose sphere is deep sleep, एकीभूतः— having become one, प्रज्ञानघनः a mass of consciousness, एव — only, आनन्दमयः full of bliss, हि — verily, आनन्दभुक् — enjoyer of the bliss, चेतोमुखः — whose face is knowledge, प्राज्ञः Prajna, तृतीयः the third, पादः quarter or foot or condition.

5. That is the state of deep sleep wherein the sleeper does not desire any objects nor does he see any dream. The third quarter or condition is the Prajna whose sphere is deep sleep, in whom all experiences have become one, who is verily a mass of consciousness, who is full of bliss, who enjoys bliss, and who is the way leading to the knowledge (of the two other states).

The Jivatma experiences deep sleep when he does not experience sound and other objects of senses by the cessa-

tion of the functions of the nineteen organs. There is no func-
tioning of the mind in this state. Egoism also is absent. But
there is *avidya*, the veil of ignorance.

Under the orders of Isvara, he who is coupled with
Avyakta, the vehicle of Maya having entered the microcosmic
Karana body, reaches the state of Prajna. He goes by the
names of Prajna, Avicchinna, Paramarthika and Sushupti
Abhimani. Just as a bird, tired of roaming, flies to its nest with
its stomach filled, so the Jiva being tired of the actions of the
world in the waking and dreaming states, enters Ajnana and
enjoys bliss.

Ekibhutah: Having become one, as in darkness all
things become one, being covered by darkness; Visva and
Taijasa have entered the condition of oneness here. The
knowledge of the wakeful and dreaming states has entered
into oneness. All the experiences of the waking and the
dream states have become one or unified with the experience of the deep sleep. They melt or dissolve or merge in the
experience of deep sleep. They are not annihilated but they
remain in a seed state, they exist in a potential state, just as a
tree exists in a seed as a unity without particularisation, without variety or manifoldness. The experiences of the wakeful
and dream states become a dense mass of consciousness
during deep sleep, Prajnanaghana.

Prajna: All-knower; he knows the past and future also.
Sarvavishaya-jnatritvam asya eva iti Prajna—who has a
knowledge of every object, according to Sri Sankara.

In deep sleep the mind is involved into its cause, the
Mula Ajnana or Avidya. There is the veil of ignorance between the individual soul and Brahman. Therefore, the Jiva
cannot attain knowledge of Brahman. The bliss enjoyed in
deep sleep state is Avidya Avrita Sukha, i.e., bliss enveloped
by ignorance.

That which is experienced only can be remembered.
There is memory of the bliss of the deep sleep state in the

waking state. When you return from sound sleep to wakefulness you remember the bliss of the deep sleep state and say:
'I slept happily, I did not know anything.' You express: 'I did
not know anything,' because you do not get any knowledge of
the Self, although you rest in Brahman. There is the veil of ignorance between you and Brahman. The remembrance of
the bliss of deep sleep state when you come back to the
wakeful state indicates that the Sakshi or the witness of three
states (viz., waking state, dream state and deep sleep state)
exists. That Sakshi is Brahman, the Supreme Self.

Anandamaya: full of bliss. This is not absolute Bliss.
This is not Bliss Infinite of the Atman. This is not the positive
transcendental and highest bliss of Brahman, of Nirvikalpa
Samadhi. The mind is in a state of quiescence as there is no
Sankalpa-vikalpa, thought and doubting. It is free from trou-
ble. This is a negative condition of happiness. There is free-
dom from unhappiness.

Chetomukha: The deep sleep forms the doorway or
gateway to the experience of waking and dream states. From
sleep you pass on to the definite cognitions of waking and
dream states. Sleep is the antecedent of the waking and
dream states.

In deep sleep one does not attain Brahmajnana, the
knowledge of the Self, because as soon as he comes to the
waking state he is still ignorant, he beholds the multpile or
manifold objects, he is affected by the external objects;
whereas a sage who returns from Samadhi has full knowledge of the Self, he perceives unity or oneness everywhere.
He is not affected by the worldly objects. This is the difference
between sleep and Samadhi.

एष सर्वेश्वर एष सर्वज्ञ एषोऽन्तर्याम्येष योनिः सर्वस्य प्रभवाप्ययौ हि
भूतानाम् ॥६॥

एषः — This, सर्वेश्वरः — Lord of all, एषः — this, सर्वज्ञः — the all-knower, एषः — this, अन्तर्यामी — the cause, एषः — this, योनिः — origin, सर्वस्य — of all, प्रभवाप्ययौ —the origin and end, हि — verily, भूतानाम् — of all beings.

6. This is the Lord of all, this is the knower of all, this is the Internal Ruler, this is the cause of all, this is verily the Origin and End of all beings.

Sarvesvara: Lord of all, i.e., the Governor of the whole physical and super-physical universe. As all the mental and physical worlds proceed from Isvara, as He is omnipotent, as He controls everything, He is called the Lord of all. Isvara is not something separate from the world. Sri Sankara has refuted the theory of the Naiyayikas who admit an extra-cosmic creator. Prajna is regarded as equal to Isvara. Just as the whole world has come out of Isvara, so also the waking and dream states have come out of deep sleep. That is the reason why in the previous Mantra it is said that the deep sleep state is the doorway or gateway to the waking and dream states. The waking and dream states dissolve also in the deep sleep state.

This Prajna is the knower of all as He is in all beings and all conditions. Hence He is called All-knowing. He is Antaryami, i.e., inner ruler, the governor of all beings, from within. He is the controller from within. He has entered into all beings and directs everything from within. He is the source or womb of all. From Him proceeds the varied universe. Therefore He is also the origin, and the place of dissolution for all beings. All beings finally disappear in Him. He is the final resort for all beings.

Isvara does not exert from outside to create the worlds. He does not want any instrument or materials to work with as a potter requires them to make a pot. He is omnipotent. He wills. Everything comes into being. He is the internal ruler. He resides or dwells within all beings and controls everything. He is the material cause as well as the instrumental or efficient cause. He projects this world and withdraws it within Himself, just as a serpent lengthens its body and coils it up, just as the lotus opens and shuts itself, just as the tortoise projects its limbs and withdraws them.

नान्तःप्रज्ञं न बहिष्प्रज्ञं नोभयतःप्रज्ञं न प्रज्ञानघनं न प्रज्ञं नाप्रज्ञम् ।
अदृष्टमव्यवहार्यमग्राह्यमलक्षणमचिन्त्यमव्यपदेश्यमेकात्मप्रत्ययसारं
प्रपञ्चोपशमं शान्तं शिवमद्वैतं चतुर्थं मन्यन्ते स आत्मा स विज्ञेयः ।।७।।

न — not, अन्तः प्रज्ञं — inwardly cognitive, न — not, बहिष्प्रज्ञं — outwardly cognitive, न — not, उभयतःप्रज्ञं — that which is conscious of both, न — not, प्रज्ञानघनं — a compact mass of knowledge, न — not, प्रज्ञं — simple consciousness, न — not, अप्रज्ञं — non-cognition, अदृष्टं — unseen, अव्यवहार्यं — unrelated, अग्राह्यं — incomprehensible, अलक्षणं — indefinable, अचिन्त्यं — unthinkable, अव्यपदेश्यं — indescribable, एकात्मप्रत्ययसारं — the sole essence of the consciousness of Self, प्रपञ्चोपशमं — with no trace of the conditioned world, शान्तं — the peaceful, शिवं — all blissful, अद्वैतं — non-dual, चतुर्थं — the fourth (foot), मन्यन्ते — the wise think, सः — He, आत्मा — Atman, सः — He, विज्ञेयः — is to be realised.

7. The wise think that the fourth, Turiya, is not that which is conscious of the internal (subjective) world, nor that which is conscious of the external (objective) world, nor that which is conscious of both, nor that which is a compact mass of knowledge, nor that which is simple consciousness, nor that which is insentient. It is unseen, unrelated, incomprehen-

sible, undefinable, unthinkable, indescribable, the sole essence of the consciousness of the Self with no trace of the conditioned world, the peaceful, all-bliss, non-dual. This is the Atman, the Self and it is to be realised.

The fourth, Turiya, cannot be described in words. It is the transcendental state that has to be realised through meditation. Therefore it is described by negative attributes.

The Atman is incomprehensible because it is beyond the reach of the senses. It is undefinable because it has neither qualities nor form, neither colour nor shape. It has neither sound nor touch, neither taste nor smell and therefore it is indescribable. The reader may doubt here as to the very existence of the Atman. Hence it is said that the Atman is the sole essence of the consciousness of Self, Existence Absolute, the Self of all, an embodiment of calmness and bliss, one without a second, partless, homogeneous essence, Akhanda-ekarasa.

Antah-prajna: knowledge of impressions as in dreams.

Bahih-prajna: consciousness of external objects.

It is Alakshanam. Therefore, it is beyond thought.

The fourth state, Turiya, is distinct from the waking state, the dreaming state, an intermediary state between waking and dreaming, and the deep sleep state. It is perfect awareness or pure Consciousness. Turiya is distinct from Isvara. Turiya or Brahman has no relation with the world, whereas Isvara governs the world. Brahman is Nirupadhika, i.e., free from the Upadhi of Maya, whereas Isvara is Sa-upadhika, i.e., with Maya. Brahman is supra-cosmic, Isvara has cosmic consciousness.

Strictly speaking Turiya is not a state. Turiya or Brahman is an embodiment of peace and bliss. It is the substratum for the other three states, viz., waking, dreaming and deep sleep. It pervades the three states. It is Existence Absolute, Knowledge Absolute and Bliss Absolute.

Turiya or Brahman cannot be grasped by the senses. Therefore it is transcendental. It is Svatasiddha, self proved. It is the basis for all proofs. It exists before the act of proving.

सोऽयमात्माऽध्यक्षरमोंकारोऽधिमात्रं पादा मात्रा मात्राश्च पादा अकार उकारो मकार इति ॥८॥

सः — That, अयं — This, आत्मा — Atman, अध्यक्षरं — from the point of view of a single syllable, ओंकारः — (is identical with) the syllable Om, अधिमात्रं — with regard to Matras or parts, · पादाः — quarters, मात्राः — are parts, मात्राः — parts, च — and, पादाः — are quarters, अकार — the letter 'A,' उकारः — the letter 'U,' मकारः — the letter 'M,' इति — thus.

8. This is that Atman even with regard to the letters (of the word Om); it is the Omkara with its parts. The quarters are the parts, and the parts the quarters. The parts of Om are 'A,' 'U' and 'M.'

In the previous Mantras the Atman has been described from the viewpoint of the states of waking, dream, sleep and Turiya. The same Atman is described from the viewpoint of the sound Urn in the following Mantras. This will help meditation on Om. Om is analysed into its constituent sound elements 'A,' 'U' and 'M' in order to identify them with the states of waking, dream and sleep. Those which constitute the quarters of the Atman are the letters of AUM, 'A,' 'U' and 'M.'

जागरितस्थानो वैश्वानरोऽकारः प्रथमा मात्रामेरादिमत्वाद्वाऽऽप्नोति ह वै सर्वान्कामानादिश्च भवति य एवं वेद ॥९॥

जागरितस्थानः — Whose sphere is the condition of waking, वैश्वानरः — the Vaisvanara, अकारः — the letter A, प्रथमा — the first, मात्रा — part, आप्तेः — on account of all-pervasiveness, आदिमत्वात् — on account of being the first, वा — or आप्नोति — attains, ह वै — verily, सर्वान् — all, कामान् — desirable objects, आदिः — the first, च — and, भवति — becomes, य — who, एवं — thus, वेद — knows.

9. The first part 'A' is Vaisvanara whose sphere is the condition of waking, on account of all-pervasiveness, or on account of being the first. He who knows this obtains verily all desires and becomes the first.

As the word Om represents the Atman, so the Matras of Om represent respectively the different conditions in which the Atman manifests itself. Matra 'A' represents Vaisvanara, the first condition. Have the symbol 'A' before you and meditate on Vaisvanara till you identify yourself with the object of meditation. Just as 'A' pervades in all the letters of the alphabets, so also Vaisvanara pervades all things of the universe. Just as 'A' is the first letter in 'AUM,' so also Vaisvanara is the first condtion of the Atman.

Sruti says, "The letter 'A' is the whole of speech." All sounds are pervaded by 'A.' In the Bhagavad Gita you will find "Aksharanam Akarosmi—of letters the letter 'A' I am" (X-33). Sruti says, "The effulgent Heaven is the head of Vaisvanara." Therefore Vaisvanara pervades the whole of this universe.

Just as 'A' is the first letter in 'AUM,' just as 'A' is the first of all sounds and letters, so also the waking state is the first of the three states. You can derive the knowledge of the other states from the waking state. The experiences of the three states form the whole experience of the universe. Therefore, the waking state pervades the whole universe. The scientists and Western philosophers have ignored the experiences of the dreaming and deep sleep states and have taken the experiences of the waking state only. Hence their data and conclusions are incorrect.

Now the benefits of knowing this identity are described. He who knows it has all his desires fulfilled. He becomes the first among the great. He becomes the first of all.

स्वप्नस्थानस्तैजस उकारो द्वितीया मात्रोत्कर्षादुभयत्वद्वोत्कर्षति ह वै ज्ञानसंततिं समानश्च भवति नास्याब्रह्मवित्कुले भवति य एवं वेद ॥१० ॥

स्वप्नस्थानः — Whose sphere of activity is the dream state, तैजसः — the Taijasa, उकारः — the letter U, द्वितीया — the second, मात्रा — part, उत्कर्षात् — on account of being superior, उभयत्वात् — on account of being in the middle, वा — or, उत्कर्षति — excels, ह वै — verily, ज्ञानसंततिं — the stream of knowledge, समानः — equal, च — and, भवति — becomes, न — not, अस्य — his, अब्रह्मवित् — a non-knower of Brahman, कुले — in the family, भवति — is born, यः — who, एवं — thus, वेद — knows.

10. Taijasa. whose sphere of activity is the dream state, is represented by the letter 'U,' the second letter of Om, on account of superiority, or on account of being in the middle. He who knows this becomes great in knowledge and the equal of all. No one ignorant of Brahman is born in his family.

The letter 'U' is as it were superior to the letter 'A.' Taijasa too is superior to Visva becuase he enjoys the ideas of the subtle dream world. His enjoyment is of a very fine, subtle and refined nature. Just as U is in between waking and sound sleep, Taijasa also is in between Visva and Prajna. He who knows this attains to supreme knowledge. He is treated equally by all. His friends and enemies regard him in the same light. His enemies do not hate him. They do not show any jealousy towards him. Anyone ignorant of Brahman is not born in his family.

सुषुप्तस्थानः प्राज्ञो मकारस्तृतीया मात्रा मितेरपीतेर्वा मिनोति ह वा इदँ
सर्वमपीतिश्च भवति य एवं वेद ॥११॥

सुषुप्तस्थानः — whose sphere is deep sleep, प्राज्ञः — Prajna, मकारः — the letter M, तृतीया — the third, मात्रा — part, मितेः — on account of its being a measure, अपीतेः — on account of absorption, वा — or मिनोति — measures ह वा — verily, इदं — this, सर्वं — all, अपीतिः — comprehends all within himself, च — and, भवति — becomes, यः — who, एवं — thus, वेद — knows.

11. Prajna, whose sphere is deep sleep, is 'M,' the third part (letter) of Om, because it is both the measure and that wherein all become one. He who knows this is able to measure all and to comprehend all within himself.

Just as a heap of rice is measured by a Prastha, a kind of measure, so also Visva and Taijasa are, as it were, measured by Prajna in Pralaya (involution) and Utpatti (evolution). Visva and Taijasa sink in Prajna during sleep and emerge out of him afterwards. This is compared to measuring by Prajna.

When the syllable Om is chanted or repeated again and again 'A' and 'U' appear to merge themselves in 'M' and come out of it again. Similarly the waking and dream states appear to merge in deep sleep (Prajna) and come out of it. Visva and Taijasa also merge in Prajna during sleep. Therefore, 'M' and Prajna are likened to a measure that is used in measuring rice or barley. Prajna is like a big vessel that contains two other vessels, viz., Visva and Taijasa. In Prajna all things lose their identity, all become one. Therefore Prajna is identical with the letter 'M.'

He who knows this is able to measure all. He is able to know the real nature of the world. He is able to penetrate into the real nature of the universe. He is also able to comprehend all within himself, i.e., to be the cause of all. He realises himself as the cause of the universe, Isvara.

अमात्रश्चतुर्थोऽव्यवहार्यः प्रपञ्चोपशमः शिवोऽद्वैत एवमोंकार आत्मैव संविशत्यात्मनाऽऽत्मानं य एवं वेद ॥१२॥

अमात्रः — Without parts, चतुर्थः — the fourth, अव्यवहार्यः — transcendental, प्रपञ्चोपशमः — destitute of phenomenal existence, शिवः — all bliss, अद्वैतः — non-dual, एवं — thus, ओंकारः — the syllable Om, आत्मा — Atman, एव — only, संविशति — enters, आत्मना — by his own Self, आत्मानं — the Self, यः — who, एवं — thus, वेद — knows, यः — who, एवं — thus, वेद — knows.

12. That which has no parts is the Fourth, transcendental, destitute of phenomenal existence, all bliss and non-dual. This verily is Omkara. He who knows this merges his self in the Self.

That which has no parts is called Amatra, without measure. Amatra Omkara is the fourth quarter, i.e., pure Atman. The benefit derived from the realisation of the Atman, the Fourth is that the knower himself enters into the Self by means of the Self. He attains immortality. He is not born again. As the Atman is beyond the reach of mind and senses, It is transcendental. Visva merges in Taijasa, Taijasa in Prajna and Prajna dissolves itself in Turiya Atman Brahman.

Meditation on Om helps the aspirant in the attainment of Self-realisation or the final realisation of Brahman. Just as the rope is realised when the illusion of snake vanishes, so also Brahman who is Om is realised when the illusion of duality or *avidya* disappears, through the attainment of knowledge of the Self.

।। इति माण्डूक्योपनिषत्संपूर्णा ।।

Thus ends the Mandukyopanishad.

ॐ भद्रं कर्णेभिः शृणुयाम देवाः भद्रं पश्येमाक्षभिर्यजत्राः । स्थिरैरंगैस्तुष्टुवाँ सस्तनूभिर्व्यशेम देवहितं यदायुः । स्वस्ति न इन्द्रो वृद्धश्रवाः स्वस्ति नः पूषा विश्ववेदाः । स्वस्ति नस्ताक्ष्यों अरिष्टनेमिः स्वस्ति नो बृहस्पतिर्दधातु ।।

ॐ शान्तिः शान्तिः शान्तिः ।।९ ।।

Om Tat Sat
Om Santih Santih Santih!